My Life

Edith Piaf
with Jean Noli

My Life

*Translated from the French
and edited by
Margaret Crosland*

PETER OWEN

London and Chester Springs PA

The drawing of Edith Piaf used on the endpapers is by Jean Cocteau

PETER OWEN PUBLISHERS
73 Kenway Road London SW5 0RE
Peter Owen books are distributed in the USA by
Dufour Editions Inc Chester Springs PA 19425–0449

First published in Great Britain 1990
© Union Général d'Editions 1964
English translation © Margaret Crosland 1990

British Library Cataloguing in Publication Data
Piaf, Edith *1915–1963*
    My life.
    1. Popular music. Singing. Piaf, Edith 1915–1963
    I. Title   II. Ma vie. English
    781.630092

    ISBN 0–7206–0797–3

Typeset by Action Typesetting Gloucester
Printed in Great Britain by Billings of Worcester

Contents

Introduction

The name Piaf is the name of a voice, an individual singing voice that created and perpetuated an atmosphere of its own. In these random recollections, which Edith Piaf dictated to the journalist Jean Noli during the last year of her life, we hear that voice again, this time her speaking voice.

She does not tell her entire story; she remembers the highlights, and goes far beyond the ghosted autobiography published in France in 1958. She tells of 'old, unhappy, far-off things', and many that were newer and happier. She tells of her good luck, her bad luck; she admits her many failings and attempts bravely to explain her self-induced sufferings. Sometimes she overcame them, sometimes not. She selects and dramatizes incidents and relationships, and perhaps she invented or misconstrued some of them. No matter if she did; this is how she saw her own life and personality, her successes and failures, her friends, lovers and husbands.

There can be no objective truth about Edith Piaf: the truth remains subjective, to be found in the indestructible reality of her songs. Sometimes in these memoirs she becomes confused and repetitive, but again, no matter. She could not escape her past and sometimes it overwhelmed her, just as her story overwhelms us. 'Nostalgia', said Simone Signoret, 'is not what it used to be', and if Piaf's songs are now part of the past, reflecting the moods and music of France from the 1930s to the 1960s, their messages are never out of date, for Piaf sang about the things that cannot change: people who are in and out of love, or lovers who are separated, lovers who mourn, lovers who hope to find each other again. During her dramatic life she was predictably drawn to songs with dramatic situations; every lyric she chose or wrote was a miniature drama in itself. 'It's the words that interest me first of all,' she once said, 'for in each song I try to make the people live.'

In these memoirs, first published soon after her death, she herself lives and talks. Her words complement her songs.

Margaret Crosland

1

Je ne regrette rien

By the time I die, so much will have been said about me that no one will know any longer what kind of person I was.

Does that matter so much? you'll ask. No, not really. But the idea hurts me. That's why, while there's still time, I want to talk about myself. At the risk of causing a scandal. At the risk too of incurring pity.

I'm lying in a hospital bed; I'm dictating these memories which crowd into my head; they attack me, surround me, submerge me. The past doesn't come close to me in any organized way. Faces and figures jostle against each other, saying, 'Me, me first!' There are moments of happiness, and then all the unhappy moments: there are more of *them*.

But whatever happens to me in future, until the day when I have to render accounts in heaven, I know very well what I'll be saying; I'll repeat to myself over and over again the words of my song: *'Non, je ne regrette rien.'*

This time I've won the battle against illness and death, but I won't always win it, and I want to draw up the balance sheet of my life. First I'll have to describe my childhood and youth. But they seem so far away, sometimes so unreal! I feel that as I talk about myself I'll be telling lies, although I won't want to.

It's the more intimate secrets that weigh heavily upon me, the ones which have reached the public in distorted versions of the truth. I want to free myself from them once and for all by confessing them, in the hope obviously that I'll be absolved from them. I want to explain, as far as one can ever explain one's own self, the woman I've been, all the women I've been: *la môme Piaf*,[1] Piaf, Edith. . . .

I've lived a terrible life, it's true. But also a marvellous life, because in the first place I loved life. And then because I've loved human beings: men, my lovers, my friends. . . . But also the unknown men and women who made up my public, the people for whom I've sung, even to the furthest limits of my strength, the people for whom I'd like to die on stage, at the end of one last song. All those passers-by who recognize my small figure, my way of walking, in the street, day and night. All that crowd who'll follow me, I hope, on the last day, for I don't like being alone. I'm frightened of solitude. That terrible solitude which takes hold of you at dawn or dusk, when you ask if there's any point in living, and why you're alive.

This is a confession, and all that I say from now on will be perhaps my last confession. What I want is for someone, after they've heard everything, to say as it was said of Mary Magdalene: 'Her many sins are forgiven, for she loved much.'

2

My Man . . . My Men

Love has always escaped me. I've never been able to keep the man I loved in my arms for very long. Every time, just when I thought I'd finally found the love of my life, everything fell apart and I found myself alone again.

Is it because I've never been what they call a pretty woman? I knew I wasn't. I suffered as a result and I needed to have my revenge! But maybe it's also because I'm not very faithful or because I'm so quickly disappointed. Sometimes it needs next to nothing, a little lie, or one word too many, to make my love vanish on the spot. And then I go away on the arm of another man from whom I expect a miracle.

I've always searched feverishly for the great love, the true love. Perhaps it's because I never wanted to resign myself to lies and to the mediocrity of most of my love affairs that I've had so many men in my life.

First of all there was P'tit Louis. I was barely sixteen when I met him. And he was seventeen. Romeo and Juliet?

Sadly, I'd gone through an odd kind of apprenticeship in life and love which hardly disposed me to romanticism. My mother had not been by my side to teach me that love could be tender, faithful, sweet, very sweet.[1] I'd spent my childhood among the poor 'girls' in a kind of brothel which my grandmother kept at Lisieux, and the day my acrobat father came to find me, what had I discovered as we went from village to village? A new mother every three months: his mistresses, who were more or less kind to me, depending on whether my songs – for I was singing already, and I did the collection – brought me money or catcalls.

This upbringing had not made me very sentimental. . . . I thought that when a boy signalled to a girl, the girl should never refuse. I thought women should behave like that. So I didn't hesitate long when P'tit Louis made a sign to me. I first met him at the Porte des Lilas. I was singing in the streets with my father. P'tit Louis was in the crowd, which surrounded us when I sang but melted away quickly as soon as I went round collecting. He was tall, fair and smiling, and he didn't go away with the others. When I came up to him with my saucer he looked right into my eyes, he whistled with admiration and then with a regal gesture he put a five-sous coin in my dish.

For days and days he followed me during my round in the faubourgs. One afternoon when my father wasn't with me, P'tit Louis came up to me, took me by the arm and said, 'Come with me. We'll live together.'

It all sounds a bit too easy, I know, like a magazine romance. My whole life sounds like an almost unbelievable romance. Yet things happened just as I'm telling them. P'tit Louis said, 'Come with me . . .' and I went, I followed him. Without a shadow of regret I left my father along with the relative security, the relative protection that he afforded me.

I followed P'tit Louis. I thought he was handsome, strong, unique. I loved him. He was a delivery boy. I went on singing. We moved into a little hotel in the rue de Belleville; it was poorly furnished. At first I cooked in old food cans. But Louis would come proudly home every day with cutlery or plates or saucepans that he'd stolen from shop displays or cafés.

We paid thirty-five francs a week for our sordid room. On Sundays we went to the cinema, the Alcazar, and P'tit Louis paid for our seats on the wooden benches, costing two francs each.

It was wonderful, perhaps simply because we were young, very young.

Soon I was expecting a baby. And then my little daughter Marcelle was born. We were as happy as kids. But I felt somehow that something was missing from that life. Something I've searched for tirelessly all my existence: the protective strength of a man, a real man.

I know very well I'm no saint; I couldn't count my lovers on the fingers of my two hands, and it would be easy to cast stones at me. But it's all because I've searched and searched for the man I could depend on all my life, the man I could trust. I've searched, but I haven't found him. Or else fate took a hand.

P'tit Louis was a kid like me. So one day I was unfaithful to P'tit Louis. With a stronger, tougher man. With 'My Legionnaire'. Oh, how I loved him, 'My Legionnaire'! Later, when I told his story to Raymond Asso he made it into a song which has become famous. For a long time I couldn't sing it without a shudder. Is that why I sang it well?[2]

I lost that legionnaire, surely because I wasn't destined for happiness. One day I left P'tit Louis to live with this man, without giving any warning, carrying my daughter in my arms. But P'tit Louis had followed me through the streets of Belleville. One day he caught up with me and took my child from me.

I felt that if I went away with my legionnaire I'd never be able to see my little girl again. I spent one last night with the man I loved and I came back to P'tit Louis. For my daughter's sake.

My legionnaire loved me. He asked to be posted to Africa and he died there.

If only my sacrifice had been of any use. Sadly, my poor little girl died soon afterwards, from meningitis.

P'tit Louis understood me very well. 'It was only her that made you stay with me,' he told me. 'Now I know I've lost you for ever. Goodbye! For me you were a dream princess. But the dream's over. Good luck.' And he went out of my life.

I was eighteen. I knew only the dregs of society; I'd seen nothing but ugliness and misery. Only P'tit Louis was different. But I found myself alone again. I soon went along the rest of the downward path; the death of my little daughter had left me with no heart to struggle back again.

I ended up in Pigalle among the bars, the pimps and the prostitutes.[3] The first man I fell in love with was a pimp. He immediately wanted me to be a prostitute. He was called Albert; he had a fine smile, black eyes and flared trousers. There was also another girl called Rosita, who 'worked' for him in the rue Blanche. He had such power over me that I'd have done anything for him. Except what he wanted me to do.

Perhaps there was a reason: I may have been flighty but I've always been too much in love with love to lower it to the level of commerce. My obstinate refusals made him angry. There were terrible quarrels between us. One evening, in a fury, he hit me. I bit him, I scratched his face, I kicked him. After we'd been fighting for an hour he was out of breath. 'All right, then,' he said. 'You can go on singing in the streets. But you'll give me thirty francs a day, like Rosita.'

I wanted that man. The deal seemed to me normal, and in one sense I had won. It was a kind of happiness. I lived for years like this in Pigalle with my man. I was just a poor girl. I didn't even imagine that one day my voice would make me famous and turn me into a star with all the spotlights of publicity upon me. I sang because I had no other way of earning my living and bringing money to my pimp. But I sang also because when I sang I was really happy. Completely happy. I learned later that this is called a vocation.

But my Albert didn't think this vocation was enough. He wanted me to have other talents! For profit, maybe, but even more so as to keep a hold over me. It was the law of the underworld. Men and women had to be compromised to prevent them escaping from the clutches of the crooks.

Like the others, I was put to work. So I didn't want to be a tart? Very well, then, my virtue, so to speak, would remain intact, but I would play another role. In future my job would be to find rich women. While I was singing in the streets I had to look out for dance halls where there were well-dressed women wearing necklaces and rings. In the evening I would report to Albert. He wrote down all the information I gave him in a little notebook and then, on Saturday and Sunday evenings, wearing his best suit, he went to the dance halls I'd told him about. As he was very good looking and full of confidence, he always succeeded in seducing his dancing partner.

At dawn he would offer to accompany his chance companion home. 'For', he would explain, 'it's a bad district.' He would take all of them, always, to the impasse Lemercier, a dark, deserted alleyway. He would press his left hand brutally over the woman's mouth to stop her crying out. He would hit her as hard as he could with his right hand, then he would snatch her necklaces, rings and money. I would wait for him at the café La Nouvelle Athènes. I would often see him arrive with a broad smile of victory and bulging pockets. We would drink champagne together all night.

But one day Albert horrified me. Along with André, one of his friends who was also a pimp, he wanted to make Nadia, a wonderful fair-haired girl, into a prostitute. Nadia was beautiful, gentle and naive. Nadia was madly in love with André. I gave her some advice: 'Go away. There's still time. Leave at once. If you don't you'll be finished.' But she didn't have the courage to leave her lover.

One evening André said to her, 'I've wasted enough time with you. If you don't work tonight Albert and I will punish you. And you'll be in such a state that no man in the world will dare to look at you without a shudder of disgust.'

Nadia came to me; she was in tears. 'I'm going to try to do what he wants, Edith. I'd rather die than lose André's love.'

I followed her through the streets of Pigalle. I saw her trying to pick up passers-by. All at once she began to run away and although I called out to her I lost her in the crowd. I never saw pretty Nadia again. Five days later her body was fished up by the river police. She had drowned herself in the Seine.

This death was a life-saving shock to me. I felt I'd been woken up in the middle of a nightmare by a blow from a fist. I realized just how low I'd sunk. That was the day when I decided, in the depths of my anguish and shame, to escape from the underworld, to climb out from the depths on my own. I wanted to be a woman like other women again. I didn't know how much courage I'd need. The underworld doesn't let you go so easily.

On the evening when I heard of Nadia's death I waited for Albert as usual at the bistrot. When he came up to me I spat in his face. 'You'll never see me again,' I told him, and while he was wiping his face I ran off.

For a few days nothing happened, and for a moment I believed in miracles – I believed that Albert had decided to let me go. But deep down I was terrified. I knew it wouldn't last. I knew things wouldn't go on like that.

One evening two men appeared beside me in the street. 'Follow us,' they said. 'Don't make a scene.' I realized what was happening to me.

They took me to a room and left me there, locking the door. I waited all night, half dead with terror. In the early morning I heard Albert's footsteps on the stairs. He opened the door and came towards me. In desperation I backed away from him. 'Coward!' I screamed at him. 'You can kill me, but I'll never go back to you!'

At that moment something incredible happened. Albert, the tough guy, threw himself down on the bed and wept. It was surely the first time in his life. I took the opportunity and vanished.

But I hadn't come to the end of my adventures with him. One evening when I was with some friends in a Pigalle bar, someone came to warn me: 'Albert's waiting for you at La Nouvelle Athènes. He wants to talk to you. If you don't go, he'll come here with his mob and there'll be a pitched battle.'

My friends didn't want me to go. They were ready to defend me. Some already had knives in their hands; others were holding bottles to use as clubs. I wanted to prevent a fight, so I stood up and announced, 'I'll go.'

Albert was waiting for me, alone, leaning against the bar counter. His henchmen were outside, their hands in their pockets, ready to intervene. He looked at me, then he said drily, 'Come back with me.' I refused. Then he took out his revolver, aimed it at me and said softly, 'If you refuse again, I'll kill you.'

'Shoot, if you're a man.' I saw his eyes harden. There

was the sound of a shot and I felt something scorch my neck.

By a miracle, I was still alive. At the very moment when Albert pressed the trigger, a man close to us had raised his arm and deflected the shot. It was too much for me. I was crazy with fear. I ran away.

All this should have made me feel disgusted with men. And in any case it should have made me rather careful. Instead of which. . . . I didn't have *le diable au corps* but I had a desperate, almost morbid need to be loved, all the more so because I felt I was ugly, wretched, so unlovable.

Then there were three men in my life all at once. Pierrot, a sailor, Léon, a spahi, and René, a former miner. I'd met Pierrot in the bar of the Hôtel Au Clair de Lune, where I was living. I'd met Léon in the street and René in a cabaret.

I achieved real miracles in order to see all three of them. I lied to them shamelessly but the one I really cared for was Pierrot. He was so gentle and patient. He tolerated all my mad ideas without much protest. When I met him I was already singing at Leplée's, at Gerny's Club. I worked, he did nothing. I earned a little money and he hadn't a bean. I remember that one day I wanted to give him a present. 'I'll buy you some new shoes,' I told him.

We went to the shoe shop together. He tried on all kinds of styles. He chose a pair of black patent-leather shoes with pointed toes. But he took size forty and at the time I thought it was more chic to have small feet. So I told him, 'I'll pay for size thirty-nine or nothing at all.' He came out groaning, wearing the shoes that were too tight. They hurt so much that he really couldn't walk in them. In the end I weakened. I said, 'I'll give you some lined slippers as well. In the street, when you're on your own, you can wear them. But when you're with me you'll wear the shoes.' And Pierrot accepted.

That trio was bound to end badly. Pierrot, Léon and René talked to each other. And they discovered that all three of them had the same woman. Léon disappeared. Pierrot stayed. But René wanted his revenge. He pursued me for years. It's not very long since I stopped being afraid of him.

His revenge began on the evening when for the first time in my life I was about to go on tour. I wanted to spend that last night in Paris with Pierrot. But René didn't want to let go of me. He spied on me. He was a big powerful man from Lille; he had a hard face; he was capable of killing.

I managed to shake him off. In the doorway of a shop I said to him, 'Wait for me here. I'll be back in a moment.'

I ran off through a second exit and joined Pierrot in his ground-floor room in the rue des Abbesses. We had the night, the whole night, to be happy. It was a terrible night! The room was in total darkness. Suddenly a car went by and threw a shadow on the ceiling, a shadow I recognized. Crazy with fear I ran to the window, and I saw René.

He was there, in the street. He was pacing up and down outside Pierrot's window. His right hand was in his pocket, the pocket where he always kept his flick knife! All night long his silhouette danced on the ceiling. All night I stayed there clutching Pierrot's arm. He wanted to go out and challenge René. 'Don't go, Pierrot,' I begged him, 'he'll kill you.' I knew very well that my Pierrot couldn't compete with René's strength.

At 7 a.m. René left. At 7.45 I got into the train that was taking me on tour to Troyes.

But René followed me about for years. I would see him sitting silent and motionless in the cabarets where I sang. He was on the platform when I arrived by train. Incapable of forgiving or forgetting.

In 1938, when I was going to make my debut at the

Alhambra, he telephoned me. I heard his voice telling me, 'You won't make your debut.'

It was a fortnight before the premiere, a fortnight of terror. But when I left the music hall after the premiere, searching, panic stricken, in the darkness for René's silhouette, nothing happened.

I remember that I went to the Mimi Pinson with some friends to celebrate my debut. Suddenly I heard an unknown voice whispering behind me, 'You're lucky, René's in prison for causing grievous bodily harm. He had a fight in a café.'

He was in prison for three years. When he came out he still bore me a grudge. And it lasted twenty years.

He'd gone back to Lille. Whenever I went to sing in that town I always saw him there, either as I left after the show, or at the restaurant where I went for supper. I could feel his eyes staring at the back of my neck. He never moved. As I went past him on my way out he whispered, his lips hardly moving, 'I've still got accounts to settle with you.'

The last time I saw him was in 1956. That evening he came towards me, slowly and quietly. He put his hand in his pocket. I was frightened. But he took his hand out again and held out to me a tuft of hair and the only photograph of my daughter Marcelle. He had stolen them in 1936; like that he had a means of permanent blackmail to make me come back to him.

'Take them,' he said that evening. 'I know now that I've lost you for ever.'

In the meantime I'd learned how to become a free woman again. Free to love.

3

I'm Unfaithful

The first man who gave me a hand, who tried to help me and not make a profit out of me, or have me as his mistress just for one night, was the librettist Raymond Asso. When he came into my life I was in a tight corner: I was accused of having killed a man.

Louis Leplée, the owner of Gerny's, the famous nightclub in the rue Pierre Charron,[1] had just been found dead. Immediately, I was the prime suspect. Why? My past, no doubt. Unfortunately for me I was not unknown to the police. By the time I was twenty I'd already spent two or three years in Pigalle – I'd been seen with pimps, thieves and petty criminals. I'd often been taken away in the police van. And at the Quai des Orfèvres[2] they still remembered Albert's attempt to shoot me.

But in the meantime I'd suddenly become famous. I'd found fame only through my voice. Through my voice and that man, Louis Leplée, who had discovered me when I was singing in the streets. He'd engaged me for his nightclub where all the top people of Paris came. When I sang, those goodtimers, those blasé people, fell silent. I was an overnight success.

Somewhere in the crowd which squeezed into this fashionable club every night was Maurice Chevalier.

Suddenly he'd stood up and shouted, 'Bravo! The girl's got everything it takes!'

My career was launched. At last I saw an end to poverty, the start of a new life, a life in which I could sing as much as I wanted and dedicate myself to this passion for singing. . . .

And all of a sudden Leplée was murdered, in mysterious circumstances, while he was in a Turkish bath.

The police did not spare me, no, I can't say they did. They clamped down on me. I was arrested, charged, and interrogated for hours.[3] When at last they released me, for lack of evidence, I was a wreck. And my career was in ruins. Every door closed in my face. People looked through me. I received mysterious threatening telephone calls. The tough guys in the underworld became hopeful again – they were trying to get me back under their control.

It was then that I remembered Raymond Asso, that tall, thin, wiry man who had once told me, 'I love you!'[4]

I'd burst out laughing. He was too gentle, too kind. I was used to the tough guys and I hadn't understood his romantic talk.

'Edith,' he'd added, 'take my telephone number. One day you'll need me. When that time comes, call me, I'll be there.'

As he left, I laughed out loud again, 'Who does he think he is? Need him! That'll be the day!'

I wasn't laughing any more. I was cornered. I'd plumbed the depths of human meanness. I dialled Raymond's number, without much hope. He would let me down, like the others. Then he came on the line.

'Raymond,' I admitted, 'you were right. I need you. I feel lost. I'm frightened. I'm going to do something stupid.'

There was a moment's silence and then I heard

Raymond's voice. He was very calm. 'Take a taxi,' he ordered. 'I'm waiting for you. Everything will be all right.'

It was really as simple as that! I took a taxi; I arrived at Raymond's place with nothing, not even a suitcase, and he changed my life.

Before that I had never opened a book. I thought reading was for middle-class people. I would just read serial stories with titles like *Seduced at Twenty*. I read them for a laugh! I revelled in silliness like some dirty little creature in the mud. I enjoyed it. And I revelled in ugliness, too. The more silly my songs, the more ugly I felt . . . and the more pleased I was. I felt a kind of evil pleasure in destruction, in destroying myself, and in spoiling everything that was beautiful. It was my way of living through despair.

Raymond transformed me. He taught me how to become a human being. It took him three years to cure me. Three years of patient affection to teach me that there was another world beyond that of prostitutes and pimps. Three years to cure me of Pigalle, of my chaotic childhood with all its attendant vice and misery. Three years to teach me to believe in love, happiness and good fortune. To become a woman and a star, not just a phenomenon with a voice that people listened to just as they might look at some rare animal on show at a fair.

And yet I deceived that wonderful man, at the very moment when it was most painful for him.

It's not easy to confess a bad deed. But it's even more painful to remember how you inflicted pain, how you couldn't stop yourself from doing it, driven by the demon that lies dormant in every one of us. A demon which awoke only too often in me.

When I left Raymond in 1939, I knew that I was made to sing about love. I'd had a triumph at the

Alhambra when I gave my first recital. I sang songs which Raymond had written for me: *Mon légionnaire, Le Fanion de la légion, Le Voyage du pauvre nègre, Je n'en connais pas la fin.* . . . Thanks to him I'd really been able to become a star and not remain a mere curiosity.

Raymond Asso had in fact been called up at the time when I fell in love with Paul Meurisse.[5] Raymond, I've already asked you to forgive me, you know it, our friends know it. But today I want to ask you to forgive me once more. You were so good, so kind! And I know that you understood that if I went from one man to another it wasn't because I was a bitch but because I was searching for a love so great that my whole life would have been transformed by it.

It has to be said that when it came to seducing me, Paul didn't beat about the bush. I was alone in Paris during the war and I was singing at The Nightclub in the rue Arsène-Houssaye. Before I came on, about midnight, I always went to have a drink at a bar called La Caravelle. Every evening there was a man there leaning casually against the bar. He was calm, elegant, nonchalant. He fascinated me.

It was Paul Meurisse. All I knew about him was that as a singer he hadn't much of a voice. He was appearing at L'Amiral, the rival nightclub to mine. Gradually we came to know each other. Paul amazed me. His good manners made me see him as the typical gentleman. And at that time what wouldn't I have done to make the conquest of a gentleman! You have to understand that before Paul no one had ever helped me into my coat, no one had ever opened a door for me, standing back to let me go through first. But he did all that better than anyone else.

One evening he made a suggestion to me: 'After the show, come and drink a glass of champagne at my place. I've invited a whole lot of friends.'

I accepted, I was thrilled. And about two in the morning we accompanied his friends back to their apartment. After that we were alone. Then, with his usual air of detachment, he made another suggestion: 'I think there's still a little champagne at home. Come and help me finish it.'

When we had finished the champagne day was breaking. Paul spoke to me, coldly. 'It's late, why don't you stay on here? In any case, that's how it will end.' Then he looked me in the eye. 'Nothing irritates me more', he said finally, 'than women who want to wait three days, a month or more, before giving in. Why make so much fuss, since in any case we like each other?'

I was disarmed, convinced, carried away. I said yes. . . . Our affair lasted two years.

What an adventure that was: chaotic, passionate, and now that I think about it again, marvellous all the same. When we separated Paul had finally lost the thing that irritated me most about him, his damnable sang-froid.

At first I often lost my temper. He never lost his. When we quarrelled it was I who looked wild and ridiculous. He didn't react. In the end I found that he was defying me. I would go up to him quietly on tiptoe without his noticing, and I'd suddenly scream loudly right in his ear. But he didn't even jump. Then I'd smash everything up. I'd throw glasses at the wall, just above his head. I threw everything I could get my hands on. I screamed, I stamped, I wept, I insulted him. Paul lay quietly on the bed, closed his eyes and put a newspaper over his face. He said only one thing: 'Don't smash the radio, please.'

Then one day, just to drive him into a rage, I broke this famous radio. As I held it in my hands Paul half-opened one eye. Then I threw the radio on the floor and stamped on it.

This time Paul, the gentleman, got up without a

word. He stood close to me. 'That wasn't a nice thing to do,' he said. Then he slapped my face and lay down on the bed again. I'd failed!

His sang-froid drove me crazy, so one evening, after a fight, I told him, 'It's all over between us, I'm leaving.'

I went to have dinner with Tino Rossi at Fouquet's, but during that dinner I could talk only about Paul. I loved him, he drove me mad, I missed him. Then Tino secretly telephoned Paul: 'We're going to the Dinarzade. Come and join her. You're the only man she's thinking about.'

But it would have been too easy – I wasn't to be had like that! When Paul arrived, my anger suddenly broke out again. In front of everyone I threatened to smash a bottle of champagne over his head. He left again, without a word. When I came out he was waiting for me in the street, beside a fiacre. There was a terrible battle. I didn't want to go with him and he tried with all his strength to make me get into the fiacre. In the end he managed to grab hold of me and force me down on the seat. As the fiacre went along at a trotting pace I yelled at the top of my voice: 'Help! Police! I'm being kidnapped!'

When we arrived home Paul laid me down on the pavement, sat on top of me and, holding on to my hands, said to the coachman, 'Take my wallet out of my pocket and pay yourself.'

When the fiacre had gone Paul dragged me up the stairs. I yelled with anger, I struggled, I kicked him. In the end he succeeded in getting me into the apartment. As soon as he let me go I rushed to the door and tried to get away again. But something stopped me.

The hard-bitten Paul, who was so infuriatingly passive, collapsed and sat on the edge of a chair. 'I can't take any more, Didou,' he murmured. 'Stop, I beg you! Stay with me!'

I was shattered and I stayed.

But our union wasn't any calmer. I'd decided to make him jealous, thinking I'd keep him closer to me. What a plague I was! I made dates with men in cafés and I could sense that Paul was following me down the street. He took amazing precautions to stop me from recognizing him. He would slip behind streetlamps, hide behind cars or in courtyard entrances. He would spy on me; he would wait for me on the pavement for hours. One day, in a fury, he burst into the café where I was sitting with another man and said, 'Come back home at once.'

I obeyed him immediately. In the street I tripped along beside him. 'Paul,' I told him, 'it was all a game. I was stupid, I wanted to make you jealous.'

But Paul didn't reply and dragged me along by my arm.

As soon as I was home he began to smash everything that I'd spared so far. Then he slapped me so hard that I had a black eye, which hurt so much I couldn't eat anything for three days.

In the end it was our profession that separated us and not our quarrels or fights. Paul was away on tour all the time, and so was I. One day we didn't meet any more. And then, quietly, without any tears or shouting, Paul became a friend to me, the most delightful of friends.

I was twenty-five. I'd lived a hectic life and yet I still didn't know what love was really like. For me it had been fighting, telling big lies, and blows. That was no doubt why, after Paul, my amorous adventures became pathetic.

There was a married composer. He was a handsome man, tall and elegant. He led me up the garden path for months. He kept on saying to me, 'Give me a month to divorce my wife. After that, I'll never leave you again.' The truth was that he hadn't the courage to get a divorce.

'If', I said to him, 'I see that you're stringing me along, I'll be unfaithful to you.'

He *was* stringing me along. I kept my word. I was unfaithful to him. The next day, I told him. But he was so conceited that he didn't want to believe me. So I picked up the telephone and called my new lover. The composer took the other receiver. When he put it down he was as white as a sheet and left.

With this sort of behaviour it was obvious what would happen in the end, and it did happen: men took me for an easy lay. I became a legend for my entourage, fair game for theatre people passing through. Men took me for granted. And yet, deep within me, I felt pure and desperate and a long way from this degrading image.

I realized how far I had fallen one day in New York when I was dining with friends in my suite at the Waldorf Astoria. I had invited John Garfield, the American film star.[6] After the meal I accompanied my other guests to the door, but when I came back to the drawing room John had disappeared. I looked for him everywhere and finally I found him, very sure of himself, lying on my bed, smoking a cigarette and completely naked. I threw his clothes in his face and chucked him out, then I flung myself on my bed in tears and swore I'd turn over a new leaf.

All this lying, all this fighting, these sordid deceptions: it all came to a bad end. Thanks to this idiotic life, I passed close to a great love and failed to see it because I didn't believe in it.

It was in Greece, in 1946 – in Athens, where I was singing. Every night, when I left the stage, I was brought a bouquet of flowers, always the same ones. I wondered who was sending them to me.

One night he came. Tall, with dark curly hair, proud and romantic. He was called Takis Menelas. He was a stage artist. He took me to the foot of the Acropolis and began to talk to me. The moonlight, the sound of singing that rose from the town and the voice of Takis beside me, a warm, vibrant voice. . . . I felt like a young girl hearing a declaration of love for the first time.

For a week I lived through a great love. Takis begged me to stay: 'Stay,' he said. 'If you go I know that I'll never see you again. Stay! For you I'll get a divorce. We'll be married. Stay! Sacrifice your fame – stay with me in this wonderful country.'

But I didn't believe him. I'd thrown away love so often myself that I didn't believe in anything any more, except perhaps in pleasure.

I saw Takis again four years later. He was staying briefly in Paris. He was on his way back from New York, where he had turned down a fabulous contract. He had turned down fame and riches because he was homesick for his own country. That day, we saw each other for barely a few minutes. His lips trembled as he spoke to me: 'I know that you don't love me any more. But I haven't forgotten you. For you, in memory of you, I've gone through a divorce.'

That day I realized that I'd passed happiness by, and it was my fault. All I'd needed was a little more confidence.

I had news of Takis Menelas during one of my recent illnesses. He sent me back a good-luck medallion which I had given him, with these simple words: 'You need it more that I do.'

And now the time has come to speak to you about the man who truly brought light into my life, the man who surely would have transformed it for ever if death had not shattered our marvellous relationship; no doubt you understand that I'm referring to the great boxing champion, Marcel Cerdan.

4

My Rival: Death

I had begun to speak of him, then I stopped. Because it's too painful for me, in spite of the time that has passed, in spite of everything that has happened in my life since then, bringing sometimes joy, sometimes sorrow. In spite of my latest love, so unexpected and so comforting. This boy, my husband, Théo ... who no doubt will help me to die one day. [1]

Yet I have to describe what it was like when Marcel and I were together. That marvellous, that incomparable love story. The story, that, when I was thirty, wiped out from my past sad stories, fights and incidents with no future. [2]

How many times did my past prevent me from sleeping? Faces moving by, faces which haunted me. My father making me sing in the streets; his mistresses who would either beat me or flatter me; P'tit Louis, my first lover; Albert, the pimp from Pigalle, with whom I lived; Leplée, the owner of Gerny's, whom I'd been accused of murdering; and Raymond Asso and Paul Meurisse – all the men I'd dallied with or the men who'd let me down.

All that hadn't always been very pleasant. That's why I have to talk about Marcel and me, today. I used to keep silent about those two years of my life. I couldn't even think about them. But I don't want to die without people knowing what it was really like between him and me. Because no end of stories have been told about us. We were watched, spied upon. Revolting things were said about us. I was accused of having stolen a husband from his wife and a father from his children. In fact people would have given a fortune to know what really existed between him and me. Since they couldn't know, they invented it.

Now I'll tell you the real story of our romance.

Yes, it's true, I loved Cerdan. More than that, I worshipped him like a god. I'd have done anything whatever for him! To keep his memory alive. To let the whole world know how generous, how wonderful he was. I wanted to shout it from the rooftops: 'Marcel Cerdan changed my life!'

Before I met him, I was nothing at all. Oh, yes, I know, I was a famous singer – very famous, even. But deep within myself I was a woman in despair. I thought that life was meaningless, that all men were beasts; I thought the best thing to do was to go on laughing it off, drinking and doing crazy things, waiting to die as soon as possible. Raymond Asso was the only man who had tried to make me see that there was another way of life. But I'd been unfaithful to him – he hadn't been strong enough to hold me. To be honest, I hadn't been in love with him. I'd just asked him to help me.

Marcel taught me how to live. He took away from me the bitterness and the taste of despair that was poisoning me, body and soul. He showed me that kindness, calm and affection existed. And then my world was filled with light.

I remember what plenty of well-intentioned people said to me at this time. 'How can you be in love with a boxer? He's a brute!'

A brute, that man who could have given them lessons in how to behave with sensitivity?

But I have to tell you that I too didn't discover Cerdan's secret straight away. I even thought that he was mean, and that's one of the faults I would criticize most in a man. For meanness isn't just a question of money, it's a question of behaviour. A man who's mean with money is also mean with love. Poor Marcel! Quite simply, he refused, when I first met him, to do something that would have been very easy for him: he refused to try and impress me.

It was in 1947, in New York. We had been introduced to each other at a cocktail party. Marcel was preparing his first American campaign; I was in the midst of rehearsing for my recital. We were two French people in New York. Two French people who knew nobody and felt bored.

It had to happen. One evening Marcel Cerdan telephoned me at my apartment at the Waldorf Astoria. He invited me to have dinner with him and I accepted straight away. I felt delighted and proud of myself. I put on my make-up with great care. I wore my most beautiful dress.

Marcel arrived and said simply: 'Come along quickly, I'm as hungry as a hunter.'

I said to myself, 'That's good! We're going to go to a good restaurant and have a real blow-out!'

In the street I trotted alongside this man who was the size of a massive wardrobe. Suddenly he pushed open a door and took me into a seedy drugstore. We sat on stools at the bar and ate pastrami, boiled salt beef. Then he offered me an ice and a beer. The whole lot cost forty cents, not quite two hundred francs. . . .

At the end of the meal I said, rather primly, 'Well, when you invite someone out, you don't exactly ruin yourself.'

He could have been angry. He just looked rather surprised at my reaction. Then he smiled: 'That's no problem!' And he took me to one of the most famous restaurants in New York, Le Gourmet. There we ate a second meal – a real one!

I only discovered Marcel's secret when we met for the second time. It was in Paris, a few months later. I had passed him in the street and saw he had a strange companion. He was with a friend, and was holding his arm. An odd friend...an Arab, who was almost blind. I was intrigued. I went with them for part of the way, and that was how I heard the whole story. This unfortunate man was one of Cerdan's childhood friends, and Marcel had decided he would save him from going blind. He had brought him to Paris, paying his fare from Casablanca, and then each morning he took him to the specialist. He looked after him affectionately and consoled him. He paid for all his medical care.

I've never seen a man care for someone with such devotion, with such a persistent urge to save him. And he succeeded in working the miracle. When he took his friend to the airport to catch the plane to North Africa, the man was cured. He had recovered his sight. As for me, I had been won over for ever. I was fascinated by so much goodness.

Cerdan, who was world champion, rich and adored, could have thought about himself a little, could have taken holidays, I don't know what else. Instead, he devoted himself to others. I learned too that for this reason he had taken on a tour of exhibition bouts in Provence instead of taking a rest after a particularly tough match. Did he do it to earn more money? No. He had made over his fee to a centre for children suffering from TB.

When I heard the news I was indignant. I cabled him from New York: 'Why did you do that? Suppose you have trouble? Who will get you out of it?'

He replied to me with a long letter: 'I went to those kids. I felt their little hands touching me and I thought, It's good to feel useful. So does money really matter?'

I could give endless examples of his amazing generosity. The one which touched me most, the one I found the most moving, is this. It happened on a day when he was fighting a match with an old boxer who didn't have a chance against him. He was just about to give the knockout punch when he heard the other man's voice: 'Let me go on, Marcel,' he begged, 'let me go on.'

So he allowed himself just to win on points and when the crowd booed him he didn't turn a hair. When he told me the story he explained his reaction: 'They booed me, but I'd never felt so happy. You see, Edith, whatever happens in life, you must always be kind to other people!'

Sometimes I resisted this idea. But he was patient and he could do what he wanted with me. One evening, outside the ABC music hall, a crowd of fans surrounded me; they wanted to kiss me, touch me and ask for my autograph. I was irritable and vain. I believed that all this admiration was just something I deserved. I pushed the people away and grumbled at them, 'Leave me in peace.' And I rushed into the car with Marcel.

We drove along for a few minutes. I felt that something wasn't quite right. Suddenly he spoke to me: 'Edith, tonight, for the first time, you've disappointed me.'

'I was tired, Marcel, I was all nerves!'

Marcel looked at me in silence. Then all at once he said, 'But the people who were waiting for your autograph were bringing you their love in exchange! Do you remember the years before you were famous, when you were waiting for these people? Just think for a moment of the day when you'll expect them – and they won't come any more.'

Since that night I've never refused an autograph to anyone, however exhausted I felt.

And one evening in New York, Cerdan brought me the happiest moment of my life. I'd been singing, and about midnight someone came to tell me that there was a fair on Coney Island. Marcel was with me. He took me cheerfully by the arm and said, 'Come on, I'll treat you to a go on the roundabout.'

We ran off like a couple of children. After the

roundabout he took me on to the scenic railway. He shouted with delight. I screamed with terror. Hundreds of people were standing round us in a group. They were calling out, 'It's Cerdan! Hip, hip, hooray!'

Marcel whispered in my ear, 'They've recognized me, and not you.'

I was feeling angry already, when someone shouted, 'Edith! Sing us *La vie en rose!*'

Then they stopped all the roundabouts, there was total silence, and I sang. When the people applauded me at the end, I turned round. Marcel looked shaken: 'What you do, Edith, is better than what I do. You bring them happiness and love.'

At these words I felt tears running down my cheeks. I, better than Cerdan! It was the finest compliment any man could pay me. A compliment I didn't think I deserved.

When I talk about Cerdan, yes, just at the mention of his name I feel better. He was greater than other men. When he was there, unbelievable things were possible.

There's one thing that so far I haven't mentioned to anyone. I didn't want the sneers of the sceptics to spoil one of my most wonderful memories of happiness.

Just once, for Cerdan, I asked Heaven for a miracle and Heaven granted my wish.

It was a few weeks before the world championship, in which he was going to challenge Tony Zale.

'Listen,' I suggested, 'tomorrow we'll go to Lisieux and pray for you to win the fight.'

In the church I prayed. I prayed to St Thérèse. 'I'm asking nothing for myself,' I begged her. 'On the contrary, leave me the suffering and the sorrow. I deserve them. But for him, for him, because you know about all his sacrifices and all the efforts he makes, for him, because everything depends on this fight, give him victory!'

A few days later I was getting ready to go to New

York, where Marcel's fight would take place. I was just
finishing my packing. My friend Ginette and her husband
Michel were with me. Suddenly we looked at each other;
we were all surprised. A strong scent of roses had spread
through my room. It lasted only a few seconds at the most.
Ginette and Michel looked everywhere; they thought a
bottle of perfume had got broken. It wasn't that. I knew
what it was. I had spent my childhood at Lisieux,[3] and I
knew that when the saint fulfilled someone's wish, she
produced a scent of roses close to them. At that moment I
knew that Marcel Cerdan would be world champion.

And yet a week later, during the match, I didn't dare
look at the ring. In the famous fourth round Tony Zale
nearly got Marcel down. I thought I would die. In the hall,
in the midst of the shouting crowd, I prayed to the saint.
I said to her, 'You promised he would win, don't forget
him.'

I prayed and I drummed with my fists on the hat of a
spectator who was sitting in front of me. When the fight
was over, when Marcel, having delivered the KO, had
acknowledged the applause from the crowd, the man in
front turned round. He held out to me his battered hat.
'Have it. It's no use to me in this state, but for you, it'll be
a souvenir of a very happy occasion.'

Outside the ring Cerdan was the most gentle of men.
I only saw him fight another man twice, both times on my
behalf. He struck one man. He gave the other a beating.

The former had told stories about me that were worse
than unpleasant. Marcel met him at the Salle Wagram one
evening when he himself was a spectator. He went up to the
man, who was looking very downcast. He walked up to him
with a cheerful smile. He said to him in a kind-hearted voice,
'You're a bastard!' Then he dealt him a fearful blow. After
that, immediately after, he begged his friends, 'Take him
away quickly, tell him to go away', for this strong man didn't

enjoy fighting — he was afraid of hurting his opponent!

The second man he wanted to knock down was a friend we had in common. A publicity man. He had written a newspaper article about Marcel and me, full of unpleasant lies. He knew what he had done. And that day he had come to see me, hoping that if he explained what he had done, I would forgive him. He had almost succeeded, for I always forgive people. At that precise moment Marcel arrived.

When he caught sight of the man who had betrayed our friendship, Marcel went white with rage. He got hold of the man's jacket by the revers. He drove him across my drawing room, hitting him as hard as he could.

The other man was moaning, 'Forgive me, Marcel. . . . Don't hit me any more, Marcel. . . . '

But Cerdan was furious. He dragged the man over to me. He gave me an order: 'Spit in his face!'

I tried to obey Cerdan, but I was terribly upset. I couldn't do it.

Then Marcel pushed him towards the door. 'Get the hell out of here, and don't let me ever see you again!'

Marcel didn't understand how anyone could be dishonest. He always left his money, his papers or his suitcases lying about, just anywhere. And the strangest thing was that nobody ever stole from him. He could not believe in human wickedness.

It was Marcel who taught me everything, everything that matters in life, everything that can let you look in the mirror without being ashamed, without blushing at the thought of your past. And what did I give him in return? Not very much.

When I first knew him I used to laugh at him, for when he was on his own, in planes or trains, he read nothing except comics, cowboy stories, strip cartoons and detective novels.

'Now look, Marcel,' I would say to him, 'you ought

to read something else.'

Patiently I put into the world champion's hands books by Gide, Steinbeck and Jack London.[4] I watched carefully to see that he wasn't hiding cartoons inside the books. At first he would look at me with a hang-dog expression and complain, 'Why are you doing this to me, Edith? Why are you forcing me to read when it's fine outside and I was thinking of going for a walk?'

But I was soon sorry that I'd had this idea. For he became a real fanatic. He began to think of nothing else except books. He would walk along the quais and do the rounds of the bouquinistes. When he was reading he thought of nothing else. When I came in, he barely noticed.

I also taught him how to dress. Before that he would just put on what he happened to find close at hand. He adored purple ties and spotted shirts. I soon put a stop to that.[5]

Even when I sang, Marcel did not leave me. From the stage I could see him standing in the wings. He listened to me. He looked after the curtains. If anyone made a sound he would be angry. He would look at me with astonishment and say to anyone who cared to listen, 'Just imagine! That little slip of a woman. . . . How does she manage to sing like that?'

This love was too wonderful for me. Horror entered my life once more. The appalling event overwhelmed me. The Paris–New York plane crashed in the Azores. Marcel Cerdan was on board. Marcel Cerdan was dead.

That night I was singing in New York, on stage at the Versailles, one of the smartest nightclubs in the city. There are no words strong enough to describe the martyrdom I was suffering. I was desperately wounded in body and soul. But I got through to the end. Before my first song I'd made an announcement: 'This evening I shall sing in memory of Marcel Cerdan. I shall sing only for him.'

Perhaps this was the reason I didn't kill myself? Not that what I did next was much better. All the same, our life doesn't belong to us; you need courage to get to the very end. In any case, since then, Marcel has never left me. Even today, when I have to take a decision, I always ask myself, 'What would Marcel do in my place?'

It's too bad for the incredulous. They'll smile. But since Marcel's death I've believed in spiritualism.[6] I believe in the warnings that come from table-turning. Have I any proof? Well, after that ghastly evening, at every spiritualist seance, the table always gave me one date, always the same date: February 17... February 17...

At each seance I would ask; 'Is it good news?' And the table replied, 'Yes.'

Finally February 17, 1950 arrived. At four o'clock in the afternoon there was a ring at my door. A young telegraph boy handed me a telegram. This is what it said: 'Edith, come to Casablanca. I want to see you.' It was signed Marinette.

It was Marinette Cerdan, Marcel's wife. I took the first plane for Casablanca. She was there at the airport, waiting for me. We fell into each other's arms. We were both in tears.

'Marinette,' I said to her, 'if I can help you, if I can replace Marcel in any small way, if you need me, I'm there, I'll always be there.'

I'd found a reason for living again. I was saved. Soon I was going to busy myself with Cerdan's son.[7]

If people don't understand this, it's because they've never loved anyone, and never lost their love because death passed that way. They limit themselves to the petty occupations of the living.

Marinette and I had been changed by one man.

39

5

My Hell: Drugs

However low you fall, you must never lose hope.

Exactly six months after Cerdan's death I sank to the bottom, deep into the abyss. In vain did I tell myself that he had not left me, that he still protected me from the other world which he now inhabited. In vain did I remind myself, over and over again, that I'd promised him to be brave. I couldn't stand it: I began to take drugs. Surely I was marked out for ever as a result.

This was on top of all the rest, all the horrible and sordid things that had already happened to me because, in any case, I'd had a bad start in life. Perhaps this is why my health has been undermined and I'll surely die before my time, although I've undergone a cure.

But drugs made my life into hell for four years. Yes, for four years I lived almost like an animal or a madwoman: nothing existed for me beyond the moment I was given my injection and felt at last the soothing effect of the drug.

My friends have seen me foaming at the mouth, clinging to the bars of my bed as I demanded my dose of morphine. They've seen me standing in the wings, injecting myself rapidly through my skirt and my stockings, for without the injection I could never have gone on stage, I could never have sung.

And yet nothing, not even my worst moments of

despair, ever stopped me from singing! The day before I die I shall still be thinking of a song. And if I had the choice I'd prefer to collapse on stage, while singing, and never get up again.

If I remember the time when I was no more than a remnant of humanity, I do so because I want to warn those who, like me, after a grief too hard to bear, try to forget through drugs or alcohol. In my case nobody tried to warn me, in fact people encouraged me along the downward path. Marcel was no longer there.

When I accepted my first injection I didn't know what was coming to me. Besides, I didn't have it deliberately in order to drug myself. Destiny, my evil destiny, lay in wait for me once more, as though it were written somewhere that whenever *la môme Piaf* was beginning to get out of trouble she was forced into it once again.

I had been involved in a car accident near Tarascon. I've often regretted that it didn't kill me. I would have been reunited with the man whom I couldn't forget.

Perhaps I hadn't suffered enough? The car was a heap of scrap iron. I was taken out, covered with cuts, and in addition I had a fractured arm and broken ribs. I found myself in a hospital bed. Each time I was moved the pain was so intense that I screamed. It was then that a nurse gave me my first injection; all at once the pain vanished and I felt amazingly happy. As soon as the effect of the injection wore off I began to suffer the pain again. I demanded another injection. They made me wait as long as possible, but the pain was so intense that in the end they gave it to me. I was lost!

However, I was taken back by ambulance to my apartment in Paris. There I no longer had a nurse to supervise me. I begged all my friends to find morphine for me. It was essential for my body now; I had become an addict.

They all refused. All except one friend, Janine.[1] She came to see me every day. She brought me my shot, hiding it in her handbag. As soon as she had closed the door I would get out of bed and go on all fours to find the syringe, which I hid in turn under my bed, inside the gramophone pick-up or behind the bath, so that my friends wouldn't find it.

Breathlessly I would order Janine, 'Give it to me quickly.' Then, half-closing my eyes, I would plunge the needle into my flesh. Immediately I felt alive again. Afterwards I used to lie stretched out on my bed, in a state of stupor but calm at last.

I spent a fortune in my search for the drug. I can't think what I would have done in order to have my daily shot, if I had not had money. But I had lots of it. I was earning millions and the drug dealers were well aware of it. They took advantage of it! I saw strange, disturbing people come to my apartment. I knew that they were robbing me. I knew that they were exploiting my weakness but I couldn't put up any resistance.

It lasted for a year. I had become unrecognizable. I had reached the point when, despite the injections and ever-stronger doses, the drug no longer satisfied me. And in any case there was no more room on my body for the injections. My thighs and my arms were covered with huge swellings.

I would probably have gone mad if, in a moment of lucidity, I had not crossed the threshold of a clinic which specialized in curing drug abuse. I remember how frightened I was when the nurse came towards me. She was so strong; I was so weak and feeble – I was a shadow of my former self! She took hold of me, undressed me, searched me and made me take a bath. I was told later that many patients who came to this kind of clinic would hide drugs in their hair or under their armpits so that they would not go short of them during their stay! I hadn't done that.

When the treatment was over I came back home. I should not have done so. I wasn't really cured. I didn't know, or rather I didn't fully understand, what was in store for me. Yet Dr Migot, who looked after me, had warned me: a cure of this sort is always followed by mental depression.

I thought I was strong enough to get over it. But I didn't manage to do so. I felt paralysed. I felt all the time that there were hands round my throat about to strangle me. Sometimes my anguish was unbearable. I had nightmares; I would wake up screaming. During the day I remained flaked out in my armchair, incapable of getting up or walking from one room to another.

Loulou Barrier, my impresario, came to see me every day. I could see from his tearful eyes how deeply he pitied me. I was a wreck.

One day I was so much aware of this that I decided to kill myself. The black joke had lasted long enough: it was time to ring down the curtain. If not, I risked spending the rest of my days in a straitjacket. I got everything ready: the glass and the poison. I only had to drink it. And at that moment a cheerful group of people burst into my apartment – simply to say goodnight to me. Once more there was a miracle in my life, at least that's what I thought it was. I didn't take the poison!

I asked to see a doctor immediately. They brought one to me.

'Listen,' I said to him, 'I've got contracts to honour, and look at me! I'm a wreck! I can barely talk. Can you do something?'

He prescribed injections for me. He said that they would stimulate me. In fact, as soon as I was given the first one I felt I had come to life again. And for a very good reason: I'd been given the drug again. The doctor didn't know about my problem and I lied to him. I pretended that I didn't know that the injections contained morphine!

They allowed me to go on stage again, to sing again, to satisfy my public and to earn the money I needed to live the way I wanted. It didn't take long this time before I was once more drugged to the hilt. Arriving at my dressing room with a swollen face and a blank look, I would put on my make-up as though in a dream. Then I'd wait for the knock on my door and the call, 'Edith, you're on.' I would send the dresser out immediately and give myself a shot.

One evening I tried to manage without it. You must cure yourself on your own, I'd thought.

It was ghastly! On stage I was blinded by the spotlights, my forehead was covered with sweat, my heart was racing madly. I had to cling to the microphone or I would have collapsed. I began to sing, but very soon I stopped short; I couldn't remember the words of my song.

There was a long silence. And then I heard shouting. The audience were jeering at me.

I burst into tears. 'It's not my fault,' I stammered. 'It's not my fault! Forgive me!'

Then, for the second time, I went back to the clinic. After four days I thought my head would burst open. I begged in vain to be given a shot. Then, during the night, in my dressing gown, I ran away from the clinic. I went past the startled porter, jumped into a taxi and went home to my apartment. To give myself a shot.

I didn't listen to my friends, who wanted to save me. I sent away the doctors, who also wanted to get me off the drug. And all at once, in spite of the wretched state which I had to admit I was in, I decided to go on tour with the Supercircus![2]

This was in May 1954. I shall never forget the next three months. The suffering I endured. I saw nothing of the towns we passed through. Not a single face from those towns has remained in my memory.

And for good reason! I was no more than a sort of

mindless puppet. Each time we left for a new place my secretary used to drag me to the car and I would immediately fall into a kind of sleepy stupor. When we arrived at the next venue they would haul me into my room and put me to bed. Then I'd wait for Janine, who went to Paris every week to bring me my new ration of the drug.

I was in such a state that on some evenings I would mix up the words of my songs or invent new ones. My musicians had to perform miracles in order to catch up with me.

The infernal tour came to an end at Cholet. After my last song Lou Barrier and my secretary wrapped me up in a blanket and carried me to my car. We drove through the night. At dawn, for the third time in three years, I entered the detoxification clinic.

Dr Migot greeted me sadly: 'You again!'

'This time,' I replied, 'it's the last time. Either I'm cured or I'll kill myself!'

During the first few days they gave me an injection whenever I asked for it. Then they reduced the number of shots. It was from that moment that my organism, which had been poisoned through and through, began to cause me suffering.

At first they had given me ten shots a day, then four. One in the morning when I woke up, a second one at noon, another in the afternoon and finally the last one before I went to sleep. But the nurses gradually replaced the drug with a harmless product. Sometimes I did not notice it, but when I felt that the injection gave me no relief I would fly into terrible rages because I was being cheated. I would sweep everything off the bedside table; I would get up and like a fury smash everything in my room until the nurses got me under control. It was horrible! I was horrible! I was like a wild animal whose prey had been taken away.

Every day I was subjected to a complete search of my

room, my clothes and my body. The staff of these clinics know only too well the diabolical tricks used by addicts to hide the poisons which first degrade them and then kill them.

At last came the final day of this third attempt at a cure. That day I was to have no injection at all. It was the longest and most horrible day of my life.

From 11 a.m. until 5 p.m., I screamed like a mad-woman. I chewed the sheets. I wept. I tossed and turned on my bed. I moaned, and I foamed at the mouth. I was mad – mad with this terrible need. My whole body cried out for the drug it wanted. A terrible struggle took place within me!

But I did want to be cured, really cured.... And I shouted out the fact; I struggled and I threw myself down on the floor, scratching it with my nails. People who have not known this martyrdom can't understand. They must think that I'm exaggerating.

Dr Migot spoke to me gently. 'Do you want an injection?' he asked. 'The last one?'

Four nurses were holding me down on my bed to stop me from throwing myself out of the window. I remember how I replied to the doctor: 'No, I hate drugs! I want to be cured!'

But how did I find the strength to call out those words? Through a supernatural presence. I insist that this was the case, even if everyone laughs at me. It was a presence that saved me *in extremis* from myself. My life has been strewn with miracles like this. Until the day no doubt when Heaven will be too exhausted to save me from one last catastrophe.

The presence: it was a face which appeared suddenly before my eyes as I writhed on my bed. It was a face which saved me this time: my mother's face.... That mother who had abandoned me when I was two months old; she whom I found again fifteen years later in a wretched room in Pigalle, stretched out on her bed, moaning, 'I want my shot. . .my shot.'

My poor lamentable mother. I tried four times to make her take a cure, but each time she slipped back into her vice again. My mother died one evening in August 1945, alone in her room, while injecting herself with an overdose of morphine.[3]

Yes, it was the face and the memory of my mother which pulled me back from the abyss, that day when I was hovering at the edge.

In the evening all my strength abandoned me. I lay motionless on my bed, my eyes closed. I could breathe only with difficulty. I thought I was dead.

Dr Migot spoke to me: 'Thank you, Edith, you are the first person I've cured of this ghastly evil. In all my professional life I've never really saved a drug addict before now and I was beginning to lose confidence in myself. You are my first victory.'

I was cured, but my sufferings were not over! I still had to live through four more stations on the way to my calvary.

The doctors had warned me: 'Take care. After the addiction is cured, a need for the drug makes itself felt again on the last days of the third, sixth, twelfth and eighteenth months afterwards.'

I awaited these days in anguish. For eight months, alone in my apartment, I lived in terror of becoming an addict again. I stayed in my darkened room; I didn't want to see anybody. But one day I opened my door and my shutters again. The sun shone into my room and I began to live once more.

6

For Better or for Worse

I had to be the one to propose marriage to my first husband. That's really typical of my love life!

Obviously there's been no shortage of men in my life. Good ones and bad ones, handsome men, ugly men. But those who wanted to marry me . . . usually I didn't love them – I didn't love them enough. And those whom I would have liked to have married, either they didn't love me or they weren't free. So at the end of every love affair I found myself more alone than ever, hurting just a little more, just enough to make my love songs more poignant. I went from one man to another, hoping passionately I could stay with one of them . . . but I didn't succeed and gradually I became a little more desperate.

When I met Jacques Pills I'd just lived through one more love affair that had come to an end. It happened after my terrible car accident near Tarascon, when I'd been taken back to my over-grand house in Boulogne. I remained alone in my bed with my arm in plaster, my broken ribs, my morphine injections and my ever-deepening unhappiness following the death of Cerdan.

A man had got into the habit of coming to see me every day for several hours and his presence did me good. He was slender and attractive; his sad expression had drawn me to him. He was a famous cyclist and I prefer not to mention his name in order to save embarrassment to his family and his children. [1]

One evening he told me, 'I love you. I know there's no sense in this because I'm married. But I can't stop myself from thinking of you.'

I loved him too. We were lovers, of course. But this new love, which lasted a year, did not bring me much real happiness. For my champion could not succeed in making up his mind. He didn't dare cause any hurt to his wife and at the same time he didn't want to give me up. So he went back to her whenever I went on tour and left her again as soon as I returned to Paris.

I loved him in spite of everything. Early every morning I would sit in my car at the edge of the lake in the Bois de Boulogne and watch my cyclist training. He would say to me, 'It's good to see a team of cyclists going by.' And I would agree. He would talk to me about his competitions, about gear ratios; he wanted me to hold the stopwatch. It wasn't very entertaining for me but I wanted to please him. I did everything he wanted.

And then one afternoon the police knocked on my door. It was the same old story: my champion had brought his things to my house and his wife had laid a complaint. I was accused of receiving! They wanted to arrest me. . . .

Our story took a turn for the worse. Now we could only meet in secret, with our coat collars turned up, taking the service staircase after car chases which were as terrifying as they were ridiculous. It was like a third-rate film. No love can hold out against such things; gradually ours faded away.

It was at this moment that Jacques Pills rang my doorbell. [2] It was May 1952. He had just come back from the US.

'I've written a song for you,' he said. 'Listen to it.'

His pianist, an unknown man called Gilbert Bécaud, sat

down at the piano, and Pills sang to me *Je t'ai dans la peau*.

I liked the song. For two weeks Pills came to the house to rehearse me. But each time, instead of working, we talked about ourselves, and we looked at each other.

I was in love again! This time I said to myself, This is it, I've found the love of my life. The man I'll be able to live with all my life! A husband at last!

But Jacques was shy. I could see clearly that he was dying to talk to me about love. His lips would part and I'd think, He's going to make a declaration. But no, his Adam's apple would tremble, he would swallow and remain silent.

This performance went on for a fortnight. In the end, as he was leaving me one evening, he said, 'I love you', and he sounded almost angry.

Then I answered him spontaneously: 'You have to prove your love, Jacques! If I asked you to marry me, would you accept?'

Jacques took me in his arms and replied, laughing like a child, 'Whenever you want! Wherever you want!'[3]

I found him absolutely adorable. . . . I shall always remember our wedding day in New York, in October 1953. Shortly before the ceremony I could see that Jacques was worried about something. He was restless; he sighed.

'You're hiding something from me,' I said.

Then, looking down at the floor, shamefaced, Jacques admitted it: 'Didou, I told you a lie.'

I was already imagining some last-minute catastrophe and I saw my happiness about to vanish. Then, with the guilty look of a schoolboy who's been found out, Jacques murmured, 'I lied to you about my age. I told you I was thirty-nine, and in fact I'm forty-six!'

Dear, dear Jacques, he had thought he had to make himself younger in order to attract me.

I had always been told that for a young girl the most wonderful day of her life was her wedding day. Had I ever been a young girl? All the same, my wedding day was really the most wonderful day of my life. I felt purified, regenerated.

I wore a pale blue dress. This scandalized many people. But I had dreamed so much about that dress! I hadn't even had a white dress for my first communion, you understand, for at that point in my life I was on the road, following my acrobat father from village to village and taking the collection after his performances. I wanted to wear a light-coloured dress on my wedding day because I wanted to wipe out memories of that wretched and sordid past. I thought I could start again from scratch. People thought I was cynical and deceitful. . . . I was just romantic and credulous.

I wore round my neck the little gold cross set with rubies, which Marlene Dietrich, my witness, had just given to me to wish me luck. I clutched this cross nervously with one hand while with the other I held Jacques's hand tightly. And I prayed feverishly: 'Dear God, only let it be true! Only let me be happy! May I never be alone again, ever. Ever!'

I was happy with Jacques. Yes, despite all my tribulations I did know the quiet happiness of young married couples. And Jacques was marvellous. He didn't try to stifle me; he'd understood that I couldn't tolerate being in a cage, that as soon as I felt shut in I would run away and smash everything; he didn't try to stop me living and thinking. Yet I think that I often made him unhappy, without wanting to. But he was as solid as a rock.

I don't know if you're like me, but when someone displeases me, when someone seems unacceptable to me, I have to tell them! Sometimes, in smart restaurants or fashionable bars, I would take a dislike to a particular face. Obviously that put Jacques in an embarrassing situation. He was so courteous! On those occasions our conversations always started in the same way. I would go on the attack, suddenly making a discovery about someone sitting at the next table.

'Don't you think that chap looks awful?'

'Yes,' Jacques would reply in a conciliatory tone, 'but be good, please. Don't go and tell him so.'

'No, I shan't be good and I'll go and tell him what I think of him.'

'Edith, please!'

'No, I can't stand the sight of him!' I would get up. Or else I would call out from my table: 'You're a horrible sight!'

Jacques would invariably smile at the person I was insulting. He made excuses to him, trying to avoid too much trouble.

For a woman of my age I really behaved like a child. It has to be said that I was not always in a normal state ... especially during the periods when I took drugs.

In the evenings, while I was having a high old time with my friends in my drawing room, Jacques would take refuge in a small corner of my apartment. He never protested or showed any irritation at the noise. He took a piano into the little room and worked there; he rehearsed on his own, singing and playing quietly.

This attitude was in no way a weakness on his part. On the contrary, after Cerdan, Jacques was the strongest, the most reliable man I ever met. Moreover, without him, I'd be dead. It was he who forced me to give up drugs. It was he who made me go three times to a clinic for a cure. And if it had been necessary he would have sent me there a fourth time.

He filled me with unlimited confidence. He was the only person to whom I recounted my whole life, without lying, without deception. I could tell him everything; he didn't judge other people – he tried to understand them. It's a rare quality, I know from experience.

But one day I knew that my happiness would not last much longer. I've always been superstitious, I admit it. Events have usually proved me right. However, at the moment when I realized that my last days of happiness had come, we were still very happy. But that day Jacques was not wearing his wedding ring. Oh, he hadn't taken it off as certain husbands do ... when they meet another woman. But for me it was a great shock, a violent shock.

The thing was, on the evening after our wedding, I had asked him to make me a promise: 'Swear to me that you'll never take off your wedding ring – it would bring us bad luck.'

And he had promised.

Now on that day, which was two years later, I was in a film being made in Vichy. And on the last day of filming I went to rejoin Jacques. He was about to go on stage. I looked at him lovingly. He smiled at me with tenderness. At that moment the dresser came into the dressing room and said, 'Don't forget to take off your wedding ring, Monsieur Pills.'

He obeyed her immediately like a man who was accustomed to making this gesture. So he had not kept his promise! He had agreed to take off his wedding ring when he went on stage to sing. I closed my eyes to avoid seeing Jacques's face become tense. I closed my eyes to hide my tears. But at that precise moment I had the terrible presentiment that our love was over, that it was rushing headlong towards catastrophe.

And I was right.

Two months later we divorced. Once again love between two stars had died, because we had not been physically together often enough to keep it going. Jacques and I did not meet any more. Our professional work separated us. I was singing at the Versailles in New York and Jacques was appearing at La Vie en Rose. No doubt it was a bad sign.

When a husband and wife don't see each other every night, they can no longer keep their love going.

In addition, for me, Jacques's presence was something I missed terribly when he wasn't there any more. So I fell into my former feeble state, a kind of unconscious weakness. And bad memories came back up into my mind like bubbles bursting on the surface of a pond. I felt alone again; I remembered again all my emotional failures, Cerdan's death. . . . And I sought consolation.

When Jacques learned that someone in my entourage was making advances to me and that I didn't dislike him, he spoke to me with such sadness in his voice that I blushed for shame.

'Didou,' he said, 'before catastrophe overwhelms us, we'd better separate.' He looked at me for a long time, kissed my hand and then added, 'It's stronger than you are, you'll always play with love.'

He wasn't altogether wrong. But I paid dearly for that game. I've wept many tears since that separation. I've suffered in body and in soul. And if I didn't now have Théo. . . .

After Jacques, my long pursuit of love began again. But it was as if I was blindfolded for a game of blind man's buff. For some time I thought it was love, but it wasn't! I broke free and I began to live again, my arms stretched out towards another man. I could mention names that have become famous, others that have remained obscure. What's the use? It's always the same old story, or nearly so.

Yet there was one young man who was very dear to me, and I was to lose him, like Cerdan, in an air crash. He was Douglas Davis. [4]

He came into my life at the moment when a man had just caused me the most intense suffering; I don't even want to mention his name any more. [5] One evening he had dealt me the most cruel blow. It was February 1958; I had just been

taken ill on stage at the Waldorf Astoria in New York. The
doctors, who had been summoned at once, issued the
following command: 'You must be operated on tomorrow.
It's very serious.'

As I lay in bed, exhausted, I asked this man a question.
He had been living close to me for a year. 'Tell me, do you
still love me?' I asked.

He didn't even look at me. 'You don't exist for me any
more,' he threw at me drily. 'You know that very well.
Life's like that.'

I was in a state of collapse. Next day I was taken to the
Presbyterian Hospital in 168th Street; I hoped I would die
during the operation.

When I regained consciousness, Loulou Barrier, my
impresario, was at my bedside. 'Loulou,' I said to him,
'there must be one nice man in the world. . . .'

Loulou tried to comfort me and then he left. He had
barely gone from my room when the telephone rang. It was
Loulou. 'I've just met the nice man you were looking for,'
he said. 'He's in the elevator. He's coming.'

On his way down Loulou had found at the reception desk
a young American painter called Doug Davis, who had
asked him shyly for permission to paint my portrait.

Doug was already knocking at my door. As I saw his
naive expression, his friendly smile, I felt that I still wanted
to laugh! Every evening, for a month, he crossed New York
on the subway in order to keep me company for two hours.
I kissed him for the first time when he arrived with five
coloured balloons floating in the air at the end of their
strings. He had carried them through the subway,
although people had laughed at him. He had bought them
for me because I had told him how red balloons had been
my childhood dream, but that my father would never buy
them for me.

That day I was taken for Doug's daughter. Patients who

had seen me go by a few days earlier, looking so small under the sheet as I was wheeled towards the operating theatre, thought that I was a child. When they saw Doug carrying his balloons they asked him, 'How is your little girl?'

Doug and I loved each other for a year. But I lost him in the stupidest way possible. During my summer tour we had a quarrel in Bordeaux. Doug left the hotel in a fury. I ran after him. I tried to find him on the station platform, but I couldn't find him in the crowd and the train left for Paris. Immediately afterwards I fell ill again. Doug was already in New York, where he was having an exhibition. When he came back to Paris we were no more than just friends.

And then, on June 3, 1962, the telephone rang. Once more a man I had loved was dead. Doug's plane had crashed at Orly, a few minutes after takeoff.

7

Yes, I'm Superstitious!

Sometimes I dictate these memoirs in a half-conscious state caused by my feverish condition and by the pain. But in the midst of this half-consciousness and pain I seem to see things more clearly, and I also see faces from the past. I even see death, which is to come. I have to talk about it.

When will mine come? I don't want to think about it. We don't know the day or the time, and it's better that way. Not that I'm afraid of death. I've begun to know its face, it has come close to me so often already! Will the next meeting be the last one? Why should I be afraid when I'm totally convinced that we go on living afterwards?[1]

Oh, yes, indeed, I know those people who laugh at me when I state my belief, or else take pity on me. They think, Poor woman, you could make her believe anything. . . . It consoles her!

Why should that upset me? Because I know! Yes, I know that death is only the start of something else. Our soul regains its freedom.

Do you want proof? Do you remember the table which kept on telling me, February 17, February 17? And the telegram from Marcel Cerdan's widow? But Marcel did not stop at bringing about this meeting. He has spoken to me.

At that period, however, I didn't believe that it was

possible to partake in a dialogue with the dead. But friends wanted to help me bear my grief, and one day they made a suggestion to me: 'Why don't you try to talk to Marcel?'

They brought a famous medium to see me. We all sat round a table; we placed our hands completely flat on it; the room was in total darkness. I was told, 'Concentrate very hard.' I obeyed, nearly choking with anxiety.

Suddenly the table moved. The legs struck the floor and dictated words. Letter by letter, the message from Marcel took shape, for it could be coming only from him!

'I'm not unhappy,' he said.

At the first seance that was all, but I emerged from it overwhelmed with joy. Soon I became impatient and I began again. And Cerdan spoke to me once more. He spoke in order to arrange the meeting with his widow whom I had never met during his lifetime. He wanted us to meet, he wanted her to forgive me and no doubt he wanted me to look after his son. Since then I've often spoken to Marcel. But sometimes his spirit is not there and I spend hours sitting in the dark. I suffer and I worry, but he doesn't come.

Marcel Cerdan is not the only one of my former friends with whom I've been able to talk after death. On another occasion I made contact with my father.

I knew a man who was a magus, an extraordinary man.

'This is what you must do,' he said. 'In a darkened room, you must set out clothing and objects which belonged to the dead person. Every day you must go there for a few minutes to pray and meditate, and to beg for him to appear. No one else apart from yourself must go into this room. One day the spirit of the dead person will come into the room and the apparition will manifest itself.'

Every day I went into that dark room and prayed for my father to appear. And one day he responded to my appeal. But I never wanted to do this again. It was too painful.

There is another reason which prevents me from being really afraid of death. I'm convinced that I've been dead already!

It happened last February when I was in the American Hospital. My personal nurse, Mamie, witnessed what I'm going to tell you. I'd been in a near-coma for several days when suddenly I regained consciousness. I opened my eyes and said to Mamie, 'Listen, an extraordinary thing has just happened to me. I've seen people who are dead, in a landscape which doesn't exist. I'm sure that for a few seconds I was with them.'

'It's true,' Mamie replied. 'For a fraction of a second your heart stopped beating and everyone thought it was the end. Then it started to beat again.'

My seance table (it's a little round table) follows me everywhere I go. My chauffeur transports it. One day it saved my life and the lives of those around me. In 1956 we were due to leave for San Francisco, but for several days the table had never stopped spelling out very firmly a date and a terrifying message: . . . March 22 . . . plane down . . . no survivors . . .

I spoke to Louis Barrier, my impresario: 'Tell me, Loulou, on March 22, will we be taking a plane?'

Loulou said yes, we would. I then ordered that no one in my group should travel by plane on March 22.

When the day came I asked Loulou, 'Has our plane arrived safely?'

Everyone thought it had and people were already looking at me sideways, as if to say, 'You see, Edith, your seance table shouldn't be taken seriously.' But when we opened the newspaper we all went white.

For that morning the plane, which should have landed at San Francisco, had come down in the sea, in the harbour roads. Not one person survived: there were sixty-seven victims.

You can think anything you like: chance, destiny, whatever you prefer. Believe what you want to believe. I myself say no. I think that one of the dead people close to me had warned me. They know what is going to happen. This has always been my experience.

Besides, I live in a world full of signs and portents, and I always take care that I don't ignore the warnings. They were seen as the dreams of a drug addict, an alcoholic...a madwoman! I'm not unaware of the remarks occasioned by admissions of this sort, and I could reply to those who are sceptical or dogmatic: 'I'm closer to death than you are. I've plunged more deeply than you have into the gulfs of suffering which come before it. One day perhaps you'll realize I was right!'

Moreover, even scientists take an interest in dreams containing premonitions; they admit their existence without finding any rational explanation for them. So why should my explanation not be the right one?

In my own case I have a dream, always the same dream, every time I'm going to stop loving the man I'm living with. In my dream I hear the telephone ringing. I answer it at once. I say, 'Hello', and there is silence, so I ask desperately, 'Answer me, talk to me, say something.' But at the other end of the line nobody answers. I hear only the sound of sobbing. Each time I wake up.

And soon afterwards, without fail, things go wrong.

On another occasion, a dream saved me when I was near to death. I had just left the American Hospital in Neuilly after the terrible illness which had struck me in July 1961. I had undergone an operation and this time I was told I had been saved. I had been sent to convalesce at Loulou's country house, near Houdan. The night after I arrived I had a dream in which an ambulance appeared. When I woke up I asked to be taken back immediately to the hospital; nobody understood why.

I besought them: 'Hurry! Hurry up, then!'

Charles Dumont and Loulou Barrier had been summoned urgently and when they arrived, wondering what this new whim was all about, they saw that my face was bathed in sweat. I was writhing in pain, clutching my stomach.

At midday, in Paris, the doctors made their diagnosis: it was an intestinal blockage. They had to operate immediately. If I had not had that dream, if I had not understood the meaning of it, I should have been dead! After that, how could I not believe in supernatural powers!

I remember endless examples of their presence in my life. Listen to this: it was about July 24, 1951. The astrologer whom I consult regularly made an announcement to me: 'You will soon have two car accidents.'

In fact on the 24th, when I was setting out on tour with Charles Aznavour, his Citroën 15 ran off the road at the Cerisiers turning in the Yonne. It literally flew up into the air, then crashed at full speed into a telegraph pole. Nothing, absolutely nothing, was left of the car. But Charles and I found ourselves lying stretched out full length in a field, safe and sound!

Three weeks later Charles and I were half asleep in the back of another car driven by the cyclist Pousse. At about eight o'clock in the morning the car skidded at a bend in the road near Tarascon. This time my left arm was broken.

And my third accident, the one that took place in September 1958 when Moustaki was driving us back to Paris, had also been foretold by a medium. That is why I was found in the wreckage of the car holding the gold cross that Marlene Dietrich had given to me on my wedding day. For whenever I received a warning, I always had this lucky-charm cross with me.

And since that time? All the illnesses I've had, all the disasters that have overtaken me, everything I endured between 1959 and 1961, I knew it was all going to happen to me. In July 1959 an astrologer said to me: 'At the moment you are in a good period, but in a few months' time you're going to suffer for many months. I've never seen death so close to you.'

He has been repeating those words since my marriage to Théo, and many other things, but I prefer not to know them. . . .

I also know which is my lucky day. It's Thursday. I will never be made to do anything important on any other day. All the contracts I've signed: always Thursday! And what about the people who have been important in my life? I always met them on a Thursday. My marriage was celebrated on a Thursday. . . .

On the other hand, one day is fatal for me: Sunday. It's always on that day that disasters have happened to me! In the same way, I've never engaged a secretary without asking her to what sign of the zodiac she belonged. Instead of asking for her references, I say, 'What is your sign?' If she replies, 'Pisces', then I engage her at once, for I'm a Sagittarius and I know that those born under my sign get on well with Pisces subjects.

And then, if I hear that someone has a name beginning with a C or an M, I prick up my ears. For people whose sur-names or Christian names begin with a C or an M have always occupied an important place in my life. Take the letter C: there have been Charles Aznavour, Charles Dumont, Constantine, Claude Leveillé, Marcel Cerdan, Maurice Chevalier (who predicted my success), Henri Contet. Under the letter M there have been Marcelle, my daughter, Paul Meurisse, Yves Montand, Félix Marten, Marguerite Monnot, Michel Rivegauche and even Moustaki. . . . [2]

Then there have been the men called Louis. They have constituted the turning points of my life. My father was called Louis, like the father of my daughter. It was

Louis Leplée who discovered me when I was singing in the streets. And my impresario, the man who saves me from ruin every time, who is always at my side whenever I suffer a hard blow, is Louis Barrier, Loulou!

I'm so superstitious that before I go on stage I carry out a rapid magical ceremony. First of all I make the sign of the cross, then I kiss the consecrated medallion that I always wear. Then I bend down and touch the wooden floor with both hands. Finally, with my index finger and my little finger, I make a rude sign to some imaginary demon and after that I touch the round table, my seance table, which I always have placed behind the curtain at the entrance to the stage. I stroke it, I hold it with all my strength until it hurts me. Only after that, only after kissing all the friends standing close to me in the wings, do I dare come forward in front of the footlights.

People think I'm hard and cynical, amusing myself with others and rejecting them when they don't interest me any longer. The truth is that in reality, despite my age, I've remained a poor, over-credulous girl, pursuing eternally the same dream: wanting to be happy, wanting to be loved! The amazing thing is that life has always managed to spoil this dream for me. So it was natural that I should search elsewhere, in the world beyond. . . . And I found what I was looking for.

I'm not what they call a true believer, accepting the moral demands of some religion or other. But my faith in something bigger, something stronger and more pure than what exists on this earth, that faith is immense. And I know that one only has to ask the 'world beyond' for signs, and it sends them, together with warnings and advice.

Once only I refused to see, listen to and obey these supernatural forces – because I was crazy about a man! He was young; he had talent and wit. I was going through a period of my life when I felt I was alone, very much alone.

And I thought I had found in him the ideal companion. Once again!

One evening I asked my table if I would be happy with my new love. The table shuddered. It thumped the floor hard. It was warning me. It was telling me never to see him again. I then asked my astrologer if he could see something in my life. He was categoric, he told me, 'There is a man in your life. You must leave him, otherwise he'll make you unhappy.'

But I was obstinate. I wanted to behave like those people who laughed at my superstitions. I kept my lover.

In spite of his velvet eyes and his tender smile he was a hard young man, cynical and bad. I've already mentioned him. I was just about to go into hospital for an operation and I asked him, 'Do you still love me just a little?'

He replied, 'Oh, leave me in peace. It's all over between us.'

Worse still, after the operation, when I was prostrate in my hospital bed, I would call him every day. I heard his voice on the telephone – for he had left me to go to Florida for a beach holiday – his mocking voice saying, 'The sunshine's marvellous. I feel great and the girls . . . the girls are wonderful. . . . '

And people are surprised that I've sometimes taken to the bottle!

If life has spared me nothing it has, at the same time, given me a great deal.

People often have a good conscience because they feel secure; they say to you, proudly, 'I'll never sink as low as that. I won't go downhill.'

Well, I would have liked to have seen them sometimes in my place. When poverty, or resentment, or my poor ruined body made me want to scream, or jump out of the window or kill someone. Perhaps, at times like these, those people too would have taken to drink, in order to forget?

8

Forgetting . . . Drinking . . .

You always drink to forget something or somebody, to forget your failures, your weaknesses, your suffering, your bad deeds. I too have taken to drink in order to forget . . . to forget that some man or other was making me unhappy. I knew that I was destroying myself, but I couldn't stop myself from doing so.

Alcohol nearly killed me. I've fought the hardest and longest fight of my life against it. Harder than my fight against all my other demons, against drugs, against poverty and degeneration.

I never laugh at those alcoholics who become wrecks. I know the hell they have gone through. I very nearly became a wreck, too, but I survived. I'm living proof that one can survive this situation.

The first time that I really got drunk was after I left the cemetery when my little daughter was buried. I went into a bistrot and I drank four pastis, one after the other, neat, from a big glass, without taking a single breath. After the last mouthful everything began to spin round in front of me. A sharp pain pierced my skull and I collapsed on the floor. I was knocked out, dead drunk. Early next morning, when I came round, I realized that whatever pain you were suffering, alcohol relieved it, alcohol made you forget. And I started drinking again straight away.

It didn't seem unusual to me. In the milieu where I was born, everyone drank. When I was a baby my grandmother gave me each morning a bottle of red wine diluted with water. To give me strength! Strength! It just succeeded, and the press have described it often enough, in making me blind . . . or nearly so, until the age of seven! And without that miracle at Lisieux. . . . It was a miracle so great that I don't dare speak of it, as though it were sacrilege to mention it.

Alcohol also seems to be a miracle sometimes, but a miracle performed by the Devil. As soon as I had discovered that drinking allowed me to forget, I was lost. I always had something to forget, hadn't I? Whether I was poor or rich. For I didn't stop drinking the day I was able to cast off poverty like an old, worn-out dress! Riches don't prevent you from suffering and from wanting to stop suffering.

The worst moment for me was surely something that happened in New York. It was due to the young man for whom I'd done so much, the one I've mentioned already. I don't want to give his name, for if someone has done me harm I let them remain anonymous.

He had just left me after a horrible, sordid scene. . . . I sang that night, as I did every night, at the Versailles. Hadn't I had the courage to sing the night Cerdan died? So why not? But when I'd finished singing I ordered champagne, lots of champagne, and I drank it with my friend Ginette and anyone who wanted some.[1] Soon everything spun round in front of me. I let myself drop to the cabaret floor and crawled across it on all fours, barking, saying 'Woof, woof!' and telling the spectators, 'I'm a dog!'

My friend Ginette walked beside me and pretended to hold me on a lead. From time to time she said to me, 'Don't bite, you bad dog!'

It was ghastly ... disgusting! Yet, at the time, I wasn't suffering.

On the other hand, whenever I was as crazy as this, I wasn't just hung over the next day, I was ashamed. I would swear I'd never drink again. I would go into a church, kneel down in front of a statue of the Virgin and say to her, 'You know why I drink. You, who know what I'm suffering, help me!' And I would promise not to drink anything for a year. But soon I would meet another man and everything would begin all over again.

Another year, in Rio de Janeiro, I quarrelled with Jacques, a musician, one of the nicest men I have ever met. I had behaved in an appalling way towards him. He had never complained for one moment, despite the pain I was inflicting on him, and all at once I despised myself for having treated him like this. So I shut myself up alone in my room with bottles of beer lined up within my reach, and I drank and drank in search of sleep and oblivion. . . .

It took me years to realize that slowly but surely I was destroying myself. At first I was rather proud of being able to drink so much. And I made everyone in my entourage drink too; if you wanted my approval you had to know how to take your drink.

One night, in Lyons, after our show, Jacques Pills and I went into a bistrot with the intention of drinking just one glass of beer. At eight o'clock next morning, while the proprietor and the waiter were snoring with their heads on a table, Jacques and I were leaning against the bar, hand in hand, both of us in a terrible state. All at once Jacques threw some coins on to the counter in order to waken the proprietor and we decided to go and have breakfast in Valence. He got into the car and took the wheel. When we arrived at the hotel he ordered eggs and white wine. We felt in excellent form and glad to be alive. I looked at Jacques and said to myself, This man is as steady as a rock. He's indestructible. In spite of last night he's clear headed and in fine shape!

At that point Jacques gave a huge yawn. Then he asked me, 'Didou, how did we get here?'

And I, like an idiot, laughed! I thought that was funny.

But one day alcohol caused me to let down my public, I who have always been ready to make any sacrifice for them. It was in 1953, at The Casino in Royat, while I was on tour. I'd been drinking all afternoon. I found myself on stage with a dry mouth, a vague expression on my face, and an unsteady walk. When the orchestra launched into my first song I thought I would never be able to cope with it. I was supposed to say, '*Marchant par-dessus les tempêtes*'. I sang, '*Marchi les blaches gourmettes*'.

Someone in the audience called out, 'What language is she singing in?' My memory had let me down. I felt as if my head were in a vice. I couldn't remember the words any more; I couldn't remember anything. It was at that moment that the audience understood. When they began to whistle I sobered up at once; I recovered my memory and I became clear headed. But I'd been frightened. . . .

After that I really decided to stop drinking. But it was too late: alcohol had poisoned me! Every time I swore never to drink again I went back on my word. I thought up insane tricks that allowed me to drink all the same, in spite of myself, in spite of the doctors, in spite of my friends.

The doctors would often order me not to swallow a single drop of alcohol again; I pretended to obey them but I followed their advice in my own way. At table I drank only mineral water. But I stuffed myself with melon in port, strawberries in wine and pineapple with kirsch. I was so impregnated with alcohol that I needed nothing more: when I got up I was unsteady on my feet.

But my true friends had decided to save me, in spite of

myself. When they were in my apartment they drank only water or coffee in order not to tempt me. Everybody went in search of bottles. They hid them or threw them away, which sent me into black rages. I would insult everybody, break everything. Suddenly I would calm down and say, 'Excuse me, I'm going to do my make-up.'

I would disappear for a few moments into my *cabinet de toilette*. When I came back, I was calm again, but my eyes were shining with an unaccustomed brilliance. By the evening I would be walking unsteadily, stammering out incomprehensible words. Nobody understood what I had done to get into such a state. Until the day when my secretary, Hélène, found empty beer cans under my bed! Then she began to search everywhere and discovered unopened bottles of beer in my medicine chest, hidden behind piles of drugs.

I was drinking without any taste for it, for no reason! I would get up during the night and creep out quietly, to avoid waking anybody. I would go out into the street, wearing my slippers and with a coat over my shoulders, in search of a bar that was open.

During these periods there was within me a kind of invincible need to destroy myself. Nothing could stop me. These crises would last two or three months. Then, when I had sunk to the bottom of my abyss, when everyone thought I was lost, suddenly I would find within myself the will to climb up the slope again. But soon I would sink down once more until I was practically out of my mind.

I've caused a lot of suffering through this vice which devoured me. The people who loved me no longer knew what to do to save me. I would hear them whispering among themselves, 'If she goes on like that, she's finished.'

Until the day in 1956 when I had an appalling dream. In my sleep my little daughter Marcelle appeared to me. She was crying. I woke with a start. I said to myself that it was I, her mother, who was making her cry. I've already told you that I believed in dreams, in life after death.

That same evening Loulou Barrier, my impresario, went with me to a clinic for alcoholics.

The next morning the nurse asked me, 'What do you usually drink?'

'White wine,' I replied, 'beer, red wine, too, and then pastis and whisky as well.'

The nurse noted all this on a record sheet. Each time she replied, 'Fine.'

The first day of my drying-out passed in total euphoria. Every half-hour they brought me something to drink, in that order – a glass of white wine, then a glass of beer, then red wine, pastis and whisky.

I found that this treatment was not very painful. By evening I was absolutely drunk. The first remark that the nurse on duty had written on my record said: 'At 2 a.m. the patient sang at the top of her voice, "I belong to you and let's be friends for ever." '

But it was a method designed to cure me. After that they gradually withdrew the alcohol. And I began to suffer.

By the end of the second week I thought that if they didn't give me a glass of something immediately I would die. For forty-eight interminable hours I screamed. I thrashed about on my bed; I was totally delirious. All round me I could see a seething mass of gnomes in white overalls, with huge grinning faces, and in front of me stood the consultant, who looked like a giant. The gnomes and the consultant brandished their fists in my face. Then they attacked me. At that moment I screamed with fear, and the vision would fade for a few seconds. Then the nightmare started again. The gnomes and the doctor reappeared. They would utter imprecations, shout, threaten me again with their fists. Even if I closed my eyes I could still see them.

It lasted two days. I thought that I was going to go mad. Nurses held me down flat on my bed and wiped away the sweat and tears that mingled on my face. I was like a puppet, shaking and shivering; I struggled and I called out, 'Protect me! The dwarfs are coming back. They're going to kill me. I beg of you, chase them away.' I pleaded for mercy and shouted, 'Help!' I prayed to Heaven for my nightmare to end and I called on death to deliver me from fear.

Suddenly, at the end of those two days, the gnomes and the doctor disappeared as though by magic. It was time. I couldn't stand it any longer. The doctor examined me and said, 'You're cured.'

I was.

From that day I've never touched alcohol.

9

Other People Exist

What nobody knows, and perhaps none of those whom I've helped out of trouble have guessed, is the real reason why I can't stop myself from helping others. All that they owe me ... they owe it perhaps more specifically to a little dead child and to the generosity of an unknown man. I would like that unknown man to read these lines; I would like him to recognize himself. His gesture has had consequences that he has surely not imagined. I think he will be pleased.

I must go back a long way in my life. But in my exhausted brain memories do not form a well-ordered list with exact dates, beginning with the oldest and ending with the most recent. The entire mixture comes back to me in a disordered state, illuminated sometimes strongly, sometimes less so.

Suddenly, when I remember myself at sixteen, I want to cry.

Now you mustn't envy me, but pity me instead. Today people see how famous I am and they say, 'What a lot of money she must have earned!' Millions, a thousand million perhaps. It's true. But I've thrown that money away. Why? because I enjoy being prodigal: I'm taking my revenge. I'm taking my revenge for having slept on the pavement when I was a child. On triumphant evenings I laugh out loud. It's because I remember my youth. I feel that I've overcome my destiny, the destiny that allowed me to be born at the bottom of the social ladder, where that ladder sinks most deeply into the mud and where hope barely exists.

But the greatest triumph does not succeed in exterminating the worst of my memories. The memory of a night when I was so poor that I tried to sell myself for ten francs. Yes, ten francs!

If you have always slept in a bed that was waiting for you in a house that was warm in winter and cool in summer. . . . If you had parents who looked after you, who made a fuss of you, who kept an eye on your health. . . . Then I'm afraid you won't understand, that you'll be shocked, that you'll criticize me more severely than ever.

And yet. . . . Try to imagine it. I was fifteen and a half when I ran away with P'tit Louis. One must live; I took a job as a housemaid. But I was no good at housework, being the daughter of an acrobat. I was sacked, once, twice, three times. . . . I broke too much china; I didn't get through enough work; I was impertinent.

Then I went to the Toppin and Marguet factory, where they made wooden-soled shoes. I earned about 200 francs a week. I varnished shoes for three months until the day I felt ill. I was taken to hospital and there a doctor told me, 'You're pregnant.'

I was dismissed; it was the rule.

But, all said and done, I was pleased that I was going to have a baby.

She was born at the Hôpital Tenon and then I found myself with P'tit Louis and our little Marcelle at the Hôtel de l'Avenir, 105 rue Orfila, in a room where there were cracks in the walls and the window faced the courtyard. The baby's nappies and clothes hung on a string across the window. Under the bed was a pile of suitcases, old papers, dirty clothes and all the dust that I swept up. But I'll say it again, P'tit Louis and I were as happy as kids to have one of our own.

Only we were broke. We left the hotel by doing a moonlight flit, going past the concierge's lodge on our hands and knees. We settled into another hotel in the rue Germain-Pilon. I left that room one night after knotting sheets together into a rope and sliding down to the ground.

Things couldn't go on the way they were! P'tit Louis was still a delivery boy. As for me, I entrusted the baby to one of my landlords and went off to sing in the streets again.

That was the start of endless wanderings. For two and a half years I don't think I ever stopped walking and begging. Or running, when the police were following me. . . .

With a girl called Zephrine and a boy called Jean, I sang in the streets, in military barracks and at fairgrounds. We earned just enough to stop ourselves dying of hunger. And we were terrified. One of us was always on the lookout, for we were all three wanted by the police. Zephrine and Jean were wanted for shoplifting; I was wanted because my father had reported me missing at the police station in the Place des Fêtes.

We would go so far away to sing that I could no longer get back home in the evening. P'tit Louis looked after the baby.

One evening we had decided to sleep in a courtyard entrance, which stank of dustbins. Zephrine, an eighteen-year-old gipsy girl, was horribly ugly and was suffering from mumps. That night it was my turn to keep watch. But I was so tired! I collapsed in a corner. Suddenly the light of a torch shone over us and at the same time a gruff voice ordered, 'Get up and follow us!'

It was the police. A sergeant and two policemen with bicycles had taken us by surprise. By luck the sergeant began to make eyes at Zephrine.

We had to get out of this at any price. Jean and I looked beseechingly at our friend. But she loved Jean and Jean loved her. The sacrifice was hard, but it was our last chance to escape imprisonment. Zephrine went off into the night with the sergeant. Before leaving he had ordered his colleagues, 'Let the others go.'

Living like this when I was young meant that I was not likely to be very virtuous. It was partly due to my pals Jean and Zephrine that I lost my first love... and my little Marcelle. Jean loved Zephrine. But one day, after a row, Zephrine went home to her gipsy family, who lived in caravans at Pantin. Jean then asked me to ask Zephrine to come back and live with him again.

I'd barely entered the caravan when the entire gipsy family attacked me. There were fifteen or so of them hitting me, insulting me and spitting at me. I was bleeding; I was bruised all over. I cried with rage. I struggled. In the end I was able to get away from them. When I reached the fence which closed off their camp I turned round and shouted, 'I'll have my revenge! I'll come back with my friends!'

I went back to Jean. I told him how I'd been punished. 'Jean,' I said to him, 'we must have our revenge!'

We went up the rue de Belleville. At each street corner, in each café, we rounded up our mates. Finally, when we reached the gipsy camp at Pantin, there were twenty of us, young men and girls who were living rough. Today people would say twenty skinheads.

The fight was terrible. They used knives and sticks, and they shouted – you could hear the victims calling out. It lasted nearly half an hour.

All at once the police appeared. When we noticed them, it was too late: we were surrounded.

The long file of prisoners moved forward slowly across the waste ground that lay outside Paris at that time. Jean, who was close to me, whispered, 'If we don't get away they'll have us in the nick for years. Hold my hand. When the right moment comes we'll run for it. Don't be afraid.'

In the distance, through the fog, the houses at Pantin looked like the cardboard scenery in a theatre. Suddenly, as we came near to a trench, Jean pulled me out of the file of prisoners. We jumped as far as we could and ran desperately across the stones, grass and rubbish. The brambles scratched my bare legs. Angry shouts and commands far behind us, revolver shots, bullets whistling through the air. It was as good as the cinema, I can assure you.

Jean dragged me down the slope. I was out of breath; I moaned, 'I can't go on. Save yourself. Leave me.'

But he obstinately went on dragging me down. In the end we reached Pantin. We hid in the back room of a café. I said to Jean, 'Come on. We'll go and take cover at P'tit Louis's place.'

It was dark now. It was raining. We crept along beside the walls, our hair stuck to our foreheads; we shivered in our wet clothes.

A creaking door, a dark, dirty room and my voice whispering to Jean, 'Go in.'

Suddenly a woman appeared, carrying a paraffin lamp, a black shawl over her shoulders, her hair tow-coloured and grey. It was Madame Georgette. She was P'tit Louis's adoptive mother. She hated me, but P'tit Louis loved her. She leaned against the doorframe. She swayed on her feet and hiccuped. She was dead drunk. She came towards me unsteadily, uttering insults. She seized the poker, but just as she was about to attack me she lost her balance and collapsed on the floor. She lay there stretched out, motionless. She had fallen with her forehead against a bucket that was standing there; blood ran over her face. She groaned. I crouched in Jean's arms; I was terrified; I didn't dare move. I didn't dare look at her or help her.

At that moment P'tit Louis came back. He looked at Madame Georgette's body, then he looked up at us and said: 'Get out!'

He didn't want to see me again; he thought that I had struck her. He came back into my life only to give me the most terrible news that any normal person can hear.

It wasn't very long since we had broken up. I was working at a *bal musette* in Pigalle, Le Tourbillon. I was doing a bit of everything. Singing, drying the glasses, sweeping the dance floor. One night someone told me that P'tit Louis was there. He was pale. 'Marcelle,' he murmured. 'She's very ill. Meningitis. . . . She's at the children's hospital . . . she's dying. . . . '

At that time meningitis was incurable. The patient was given a lumbar puncture, then there was a nine-day wait. If the patient survived for that time he was saved. If not. . .

For eight days I believed in miracles. Just before the ninth day, in the middle of the night, I had some sort of presentiment. I set out on foot from my hotel in Belleville, for I had not a sou in my pocket, and walked to the hospital. I succeeded in reaching Marcelle's bedside. An old nurse who was fond of me greeted me.

'She's regained consciousness,' she said. 'Her temperature's down. I think she'll pull through.'

I went over to my little daughter. Marcelle opened her big blue eyes and for the first time since she had been ill she recognized me. She called out to me, 'Maman, come close to me. Stay close to me.'

I cried; I smothered her with kisses. About five in the morning I had to leave her. At noon I came back with P'tit Louis. I was cheerful; I thought the nightmare was over.

Marcelle was dead. . . .

Neither P'tit Louis nor I had a single sou with which to buy her a wreath. We separated without a word. I went back to Pigalle. I was in a state of collapse. One of the professional hostesses at the nightclub spoke to me: 'Don't worry, we'll make a collection for you. You'll see, we'll find the money for you.'

I couldn't pay for my daughter's burial.

All my mates, the men and the girls, were as poor as me; they gave what they could. But I saw that I was still short of ten francs.

It was four o'clock in the morning. Wearing my coat that was too long and worn at the elbows, I went out into the night. I was thinking about Marcelle, about my un-happiness, about the ten francs I hadn't got. I was walking along slowly, dragging my feet.

Suddenly I heard a voice behind me asking, 'What does it cost to go to bed with you, kid?' It was a tall man; he smiled cynically; he was trying to pick me up; he took me for a streetwalker.

Normally I would have sworn at him and hit him. But that night, thinking only of my distress, horrified at what I was going to do, I answered the unknown man, 'It costs ten francs.'

He took me by the arm and drew me rapidly into a wretched hotel. I climbed the stairs, preceded by the night porter, who did not say a word. I could feel the man's breath on the back of my neck. I said to myself, It's not possible. You're not going to do this.

I found myself in a bedroom with the tall man standing in front of me. 'There you are, then, here's your ten francs.'

He placed the silver coin on a table. He looked at me. He put his hands on my shoulders. Then, at that precise moment, I realized that I could never give in to this man. If I did I would be disgusted with myself for ever.

The unknown man looked at me coldly. 'Well?' he said. 'What are you waiting for?'

I burst into tears and told him my wretched story: the death of my daughter, the money for the burial, the missing ten francs. . . . I saw that he felt sorry for me, and that he would let me go without asking what he had paid for.

He shrugged his shoulders. 'Well,' he said, 'be brave, kid! Life's no fun, is it?'

It's in memory of that unknown man that I've got other people out of trouble, whenever I could, and asked nothing from them. If that man had treated me as a tart . . . perhaps I would never have been capable of a disinterested act, one of those acts that can save a body or a soul at the last moment. I'm still grateful to that man today for helping me to become generous. Nothing has ever given me purer delight than being able to give without expecting anything in return. [1]

10

The Money That I've Earned

I'm talking all the time about love, about the men I've been with, then left, or the men who've left me. As if my emotional life alone and nothing else could touch other people! It's because for me the only real thing in my life has been love, and my songs. But for me, my songs are also love. For other people, though, they are all the money they've earned for me. And I know what people say: 'Whatever must Piaf have earned! She must have a nice bit of money put away. She needn't worry about her old age!'

That's how it ought to be, I agree. In fact I've earned a great fortune, millions, more than a thousand million perhaps, I've already said so. I've received fabulous fees; my records alone earn me more than thirty million francs, in old money, a year. In New York I was worth a million for one evening!

Yes, I should possess the fortune of someone like Maurice Chevalier or Fernandel. . . . But the unbelievable fact is this: I have hardly anything left, just enough to live on for a few more months. And if I were never to sing again I would have difficulty in living decently.

Only I have no right to complain. If I've thrown away a fortune, it's been my fault entirely – it's because of my mania for grand, excessive gestures. I'm not very proud to admit it. For if I hadn't wasted money so often I could have carried out so much good round about me!

For instance, in order to please a man whom I knew to be vain, at a certain period I bought some very beautiful jewellery. Of course it did not make me more beautiful, but it dazzled him. And that was all I wanted. It didn't prevent him from leaving me, naturally! To be more precise, he just dropped me, and in terrible circumstances. I was disgusted. So do you know what I did? I took my necklace, my two rings, my bracelet and a clip and I threw them into the WC. Out of sheer fury! A fortune disappeared down the drain!

It would be difficult to do anything more stupid and you must think that I deserve to be slapped? Yes, I do. But when I'm angry I have no self-control.

Naturally I've also wasted a lot of money with the *grands coûturiers*. You always believe that a dress designed by Dior or Balmain is going to wipe out the mistakes of nature! Unfortunately not. When I went to the fashion houses I was the ideal prey for the sales staff. They would come up to me and each time they would say, 'Madame, how this fabric suits you!' or else, 'This colour is really you!' And every time I would reply, 'I'll have it.'

In less than an hour I had spent three or four million francs. As for the gowns, I never wore them! As soon as they had left the couture houses they lost their magic and I would go back to my classic little black dresses.

There was also the disastrous business of my house at Boulogne-sur-Seine. I had bought it for seventeen million and I'd spent a fortune to have it decorated by the greatest designer in Paris. I had an amazing drawing room, and a dream bedroom entirely in blue satin. But I never slept in this bedroom. . . . It was too beautiful, too big, too rich for me. I was not used to that sort of thing. I didn't feel at ease. I preferred to use the concierge's lodge! A lodge that had been barely repainted, and barely furnished. But I felt safe there and it amused me to play with the cord. In the end, three years later, I sold my house. At a loss, naturally. I received only ten million francs.

It's always the same with me. People think, It's Edith Piaf, she's got money. We can ask what we like. I'm so naive and stupid it would make you cry; I always buy under the impression that I'm doing good business. I sell at any old price.

A few years ago I said to myself, I'm going to rear cows. It was the fashion in my circle. All the stage people were taking up farming.

I lost almost everything on that deal. At Le Hallier, near Dreux, I bought a farm for fifteen million francs. In four years it produced two kilos of haricots verts, a pound of strawberries and a few tomatoes. We reared two hens, a rabbit . . . and all the cats from round about. The central heating cost me more than a million and a half. But it never worked. Whenever I wanted to take a bath my cook, Suzanne, would heat huge saucepans of water over a wood fire. It was so cold at my farm that I never went there in winter. I sold it all for nothing when I was at death's door and I hadn't a sou left with which to pay the nursing home and the doctors!

The sad thing is that I never think, either, about what things cost. One day, for instance, I fell ill in Stockholm. I felt dizzy and sick. I was in such a panic at the idea of dying far away from Paris that I hired a DC 4 just for myself! It was obviously ridiculous and cost me the grand total of two and a half million.

It's always the same story. Louis Barrier (my faithful Loulou), my impresario, would tear his hair when he looked at my bank account; there was never anything in it.

But I would shrug my shoulders. 'Don't worry!' I'd say to him. 'Miracles do happen.'

In actual fact I earned money too easily. In 1957, in New York, when I left the clinic, I found all my musicians very depressed. Loulou gave me the sad news: the fees charged by the clinic – three million – had left us all broke. The musicians were eating canned food and earned enough to live on by playing in dance halls. Nobody had enough money to pay their fare back home!

I could hardly stand. But I only had to sing two evenings to put us back on an even keel again.

When we reached Paris, Loulou sank down into a chair. 'Edith,' he said, 'this can't go on. We must make some economies.'

I burst out laughing. 'Economies! Whatever next, a money box? This evening we'll invite all the musicians round and we'll celebrate!'

I had just opened the envelope on top of the pile of letters that had arrived during my absence. It was a letter from my record company. With it was a cheque for ten million. . . .

Loulou was overwhelmed; he gazed at me without saying a word. Poor Loulou! Being my treasurer, my mentor, was obviously no sinecure!

But it wasn't only my whims which ruined me. On top of that I've often wasted money on behalf of my friends. That's something I don't regret.

In my house at Boulogne I would have eight people staying at a time. My friends would sleep on camp beds, inflatable mattresses, divans or in two armchairs facing each other. My drawing room looked like a dormitory! There were composers, librettists, singers. We worked, chatted and lived it up until dawn, when we went to bed.

Yes, I've always enjoyed being generous towards my colleagues. Who else would I have helped? And giving pleasure to others warms your heart so much! How could I ever account for the gifts I've given, great and small? I think I've even given cars, just like that, for no reason, to young men, just because they were good chaps, they'd been nice to me, and also because I like to see sudden joy on the faces of others. Perhaps it's because I've been so deprived of happiness myself that I need to act like Father Christmas?

Now, have I been paid back in return? Let's be frank. No. It's inevitable, moreover. I've no resentment towards anyone. In any case I don't regret the help I gave to one friend. You all know him because he's one of the greatest composers of today: Charles Aznavour.

We met by seeing each other through the window. He was living opposite me. He would sing, accompanying himself on the piano. He sang beautifully. I leaned out of the window. We chatted. When I found out that he didn't have a bean I said to him, 'Come and live in my house.'

When I realized he was unhappy because he had an ugly nose I began to laugh. 'Don't worry, I'll pay for you to have a new one, old chap.'

He didn't forget. On the evening when he became famous, while everyone was acclaiming him, he shut himself in his dressing room and wrote to me: 'Edith, I've won through at last. I wanted you to know that all the applause I've received I owe to you – I want you to have it.'

I kept that letter. Poor Charles, how happy he was on the evening when he was able to invite me to dinner for the first time! At that period he was enjoying a triumphant success at the Alhambra. We went to have supper together with some friends. And I saw him paying the bill while we were still eating.

'I've waited years', he admitted to me later, 'to do this. When I was in a spot I always said to myself: later, I shall invite Edith out!'

Now he's richer than I am. . . .

If money has always slipped through my fingers I haven't always thrown it away stupidly. I think I've said enough unpleasant things about myself to be allowed this little onset of vanity.

Once, a few years ago, I was singing at the ABC. I went out one evening to drink coffee at a bar just a stone's throw from the music hall. I was leaning against the counter when I saw a woman enveloped in a raincoat go along the street. She was carrying a bundle in her arms. This fleeting apparition would not have attracted my attention if I had not seen the young woman's expression. She looked hunted, desperate!

I didn't move. I wondered what could be tormenting her to that extent when suddenly she came back past the café again. She was walking away quickly. She seemed to be making an escape and her arms were empty. I went out. I went down the dark alleyway, looking into every nook and cranny. All at once, in the corner of a doorway, I found the bundle. It was a little fruit carton, lined with bits of rag. And in it, sleeping like an angel, was a newborn baby!

I turned on my heel and ran like a maniac. By luck I found the unhappy young woman. I caught hold of her arm. 'Go back for her,' I ordered her. 'You should be ashamed of what you've done.' I insulted her and she began to cry.

'Don't call the police,' she begged. 'Don't call them, I beseech you. . . . ' she kept on repeating.

I took her back to the alley. I placed her child in her arms and made her tell me her story. It was the usual story, of course. She had been seduced; she had had this baby. The father had abandoned her and she had been thrown out by her family without a single sou.

I began to cry in my turn. She was so young. She was not yet nineteen! She was thin and small. I said, 'Wait for me here.' I went back to my dressing room; I wrote out a cheque. I came down again as fast as I could. I put the cheque in her hands. 'Never despair again. If one day you need something, knock at my door. It will be opened and my house will be yours.'

She looked at the cheque and she saw: a million francs! I heard her say, 'Oh, madame! Madame!'... Then she fled.

But two years later she wrote to me. She had got married. She had called her little daughter Edith. In the envelope was a lucky medallion with two words only engraved on the back: 'Thank you'. I still have this medallion.

And yet once in my life I was mean. But I was so severely punished for it that it became no doubt the cause of my crazy generosity. It happened during the Occupation. I had a debt to repay. A vast debt! But I wasn't worried about it. The fee from a new engagement would allow me to discharge it easily. Unfortunately, on the very evening I was due to make my debut ... the Germans closed the cabaret where I was appearing! In a panic I wondered where to find this huge sum I needed. Then I remembered what one of my old admirers had once said to me: 'If you ever need anything, no matter what, you can always ask me.'

I went to see him. I told him the story. The next day he invited me to lunch and gave me the total amount of my debt.

I began to sing again; I paid back my benefactor and then peace returned. I began to earn a lot of money again. For the first time in my life I bought gold bars, which I looked at during the night and hid under my bed.

And then one day the man who had come to my rescue during the war telephoned me: 'Edith, I'm setting up a marvellous business but I'm short of a certain sum of money. Can you, in your turn, help me?'

I knew that he would repay me as soon as he could. I had only to sell my gold in order to settle the matter. But those diabolical gold bars fascinated me. So, aware that I was behaving shamefully, I replied to my saviour: 'No, I'm sorry. I can't.' And I hung up.

I'm forced to believe in immanent justice, for this famous gold slipped through my fingers without any hope of its return!

Two weeks later, the man with whom I was living at that time left my house without a word of warning. He took with him not only my illusions but all my gold, those horrible gold ingots. I didn't lodge a complaint over this theft. I thought that God was punishing me for having sinned just once, the only time in my life, against the finest virtue in the world: generosity!

11

Singing to Live

My songs! How can I talk about my songs? Men, however
much I've loved them . . . they were still 'the others'. My
songs are myself, my flesh, my blood, my head, my heart,
my soul. Yes, how can I talk about them?

I think I can only do so by talking about the others: the
others whom I've helped to become great singers too,
adored by the public. By talking also about the talent that I
discovered in unknown people, so that I felt obliged, by
some irresistible force, to propel them along the road to
success. And, in connection with this, I shall also talk about
friendship.

People only lend to the rich, I know. In this way I have
been lent many lovers. I think I have made my confessions
boldly enough for people to believe me when I say, 'No,
that man was not my lover. But it's true, I did everything I
could to make him successful!' Why? Simply because he
had talent.

It's true, I've moved mountains, I've compromised
myself for the men I wanted to launch. But I'm glad to have
taken risks for my friends; if I die before they do, when their
names are in lights over the doors of the music halls . . . it
will seem in a small way that *my* name is there.

Since up till now I've led a chaotic emotional life,
gossip has not spared me, though I'm not particularly

beautiful. But whenever I was seen with a man we were immediately described as lovers – as if there could be no other relationship between a man and a woman.

I believe there is. Let people add to the list of those I have loved the names of those whom I've supported totally with my friendship. Come on, then! Montand, Aznavour, Eddie Constantine, Félix Marten, Charles Dumont .... The last one is my husband, Théo, but that's another story, and I'm keeping it for the end. Oh, I forgot: the Compagnons de la Chanson. Even so, I don't want to be credited with seven lovers all at the same time! [1]

It's about Yves Montand in fact that I want to talk most. [2] I think that my sincerity until now guarantees what I shall say next. I'd like to set the record straight.

What happened between Yves Montand and me? Well, at first I couldn't stand him. I saw him as one of those minor performers without any style who came up to Paris in 1944. He sang cowboy songs and imitated Charles Trenet. I thought he looked like a would-be tough guy. He seemed so pleased with himself that he made me angry.

'I don't know what you see in him,' I would say to other people. 'He sings badly, he dances badly, he's got no sense of rhythm. That man's just nothing.'

But one day there was a gap in the first part of the programme I was presenting at that time and I allowed myself to be persuaded by people who recommended him to me.

'You'll see,' they insisted. 'He's got terrific qualities.'

I was half convinced and in the end I went to listen to him. I hadn't told him in advance. I understood at once the sort of performer he could really be.

So, at the end of his turn, I went to his dressing room. And I said *mea culpa*. 'Now listen to me,' I went on. 'I always know how to admit that I'm wrong. Well, I was wrong to run you down. If you work, if you want to follow my advice, if you agree to obey me blindly, if you change your style and stop singing songs from the Far West, within a year you'll be the great revelation of the postwar music hall. This is my promise to you.'

That's the main thing that Yves owes me: I made him change his repertoire. When they start out on a singing career, these young men are all the same: they do comic acts or sing cynical songs in order to dazzle their audiences.

'You don't dazzle anyone,' I always told them. 'There's only one kind of beautiful song, a love song!'

That day Yves Montand did not seem thrilled by my offer. He accepted, of course, he could not do anything else, but he showed no wild enthusiasm. The fact is that he did not care for my style, either. The *chanteuses réalistes* just made him laugh.

The next evening, however, when he had heard my new programme, he came to my dressing room and now he made me a promise: 'Edith Piaf, I'll listen to you.'

I realized that he too had come to listen to me in secret, and he had been moved.

But the results were at times dramatic. He had already acquired something of a name for himself and when he suddenly changed his style some of his fans were disappointed. They couldn't recognize him any more. During a practice tour through the French provinces he was booed. His former admirers shouted at him; they wanted him to sing cowboy songs and they whistled in disapproval. Unmoved, but deeply hurt, he would look into the wings, where I was standing. At the end, when the curtain had finally come down and let him off the hook, he was sarcastic.

'Are you pleased, Didou?' he said to me. 'You've won, haven't you?'

But a little later he added, 'It doesn't matter. I have a feeling you're right.'

Gradually a strange relationship developed between us. Yves was like a little boy jealous of his teacher; he became jealous, very jealous, of me when I was not giving him my whole attention. I could no longer do anything. He watched me the entire time. He was furiously angry when any man came too close to me. He would be scornful about him.

'Don't you see?' he would say. 'He's useless. You're going to waste your time again. It'll be one more disappointment.'

I thought he was exaggerating. 'Listen, it's my life, isn't it?' I would reply. 'I do what I like. Do I interfere in your life?'

Gradually, in spite of everything, it began to amuse me to see this big chap watch over me like a bodyguard, devoted, but shocked. I would make imaginary telephone calls and look at his face. I pretended to hide letters and took care that he saw them. When he was waiting for me in the drawing room I used to arrive late on purpose. It wasn't very clever, I admit. I'm no angel, everyone has known that for a long time. Since he put up with all my tiresome tricks, I began to lay it on thick. I told him the story of my life.

At that period two very handsome young men were making advances to me . . . and I didn't know which one to choose, for I must admit to my shame that I liked both of them. One evening, when I was in the salon with one of them, the other rang my doorbell. In order to prevent a row I pushed the one who was with me into a cupboard. He stayed there locked up for four hours. During that time the other one said to me, with a suspicious expression, 'Some strange things are going on here.'

I protested in vain; he didn't believe me. Until the moment when he decided to search the apartment. That gave me time to open the cupboard and say to my prisoner, 'Get out through the window, quickly.' He did so. He jumped down from the first floor.

When I told this story to Yves, he merely replied, 'If it had been me I would have strangled you!'

I burst out laughing, but I should have understood that

you don't play that sort of game with men like Yves ...
without running serious risks. I almost had such an
experience myself.

Yves didn't like Henri Contet. They both detested
each other and in the end I had promised Yves that I would
never see Henri again. But one morning, when I thought
that Yves was rehearsing in the salon, the telephone rang. I
hid in the hall and put my hand over my mouth to keep the
sound down.

'That's OK, Henri, I'll expect you at three o'clock.'

At this precise moment, Yves arrived.

'Nothing serious?' he asked.

I shook my head. He appeared very calm. He talked to
me about his programme. I listened to him and wondered
what pretext I could find to make him leave before the time
of my secret meeting with Henri. Suddenly he solved the
problem for me. 'If you don't mind,' he said, 'I'm just
going out for an hour.'

And he went. At least, so I thought. I heard his footsteps
disappear down the hall, then I heard the door open and close.
I was relieved, and waited for Henri to ring the bell.

When he arrived we went into the small salon. We
chatted and joked. We talked about Yves.

'He hasn't any talent,' Henri told me. 'He'll never do
anything. He's nothing but a little boy scout!'

And just to amuse myself, I agreed with him. 'You're
right, Henri. He's a failure! I really think I've made a
mistake.'

Henri was delighted and when he left he also made me
promise never to see Yves again: 'You're wasting your
time. Your Yves will never fill a theatre!'

I went back to my salon and there I nearly died of
shame. Yves Montand was waiting for me, motionless and
livid. His hand was bleeding, for he had been holding his
glass so tightly that he had broken it.

'Don't do that again,' he said to me in a toneless voice, 'because next time I won't be able to restrain myself. You've had a lucky escape. I wanted to kill you.'

That was obvious. I stopped playing games with him. In order to be forgiven I swore to him that he would become a big star. It wasn't very difficult. He wanted it even more than I did. And he had what it needed. Nothing could stop him.

He would telephone me at 4 a.m. and tell me, 'You know, Edith, I've discovered a marvellous gesture I can make.' And a few minutes later he would arrive to ask my opinion of it.

From the start I had warned him, 'Your diction is bad.' After that he would recite poetry for hours or sing in front of the mirror, holding a pencil in his mouth. Don't laugh. Try it instead – you'll see!

He would stay for hours in my apartment rehearsing and miming his programme. I would correct the gestures he made. I would correct his voice. I taught him how to present himself, how to bow. But in his eyes it was never perfect. He is one of the few men whom I've seen work for ten hours at a time. He had, and he still has, an amazing capacity for work. And above all there was something in him so strong, so straightforward, that one was obliged to respect it. Even I did not dare to laugh at him for long.

Finally he made his debut in my show by appearing at the end of the first part, just before me. He sang *Battling Joe*, *La grande Lili* and two songs that I had written for him: *Elle a des yeux* and *Mais qu'est-ce que j'ai à tant l'aimer?* He was literally a huge success. He was applauded so much he could not succeed in leaving the stage, and even I, coming after him, had to work hard to win attention.

But I was happy. 'You're ready,' I told him. 'You can be top of the bill now.'

And we prepared his big debut as a star at the Théâtre de l'Etoile. He worked like a slave to perfect himself.

During the week preceding the premiere I personally telephoned all the people who mattered in Paris to invite them. I shut myself in my room and made more than 400 telephone calls.

'I'm presenting a young man – he's making his debut. Come, and you'll hear him sing.'

Our nerves were stretched to breaking point. Yves and I knew that we were creating his destiny, win or lose. A few hours before he was due to go on stage, I took him by the hand and said, 'Yves, come with me – we're going to pray for you.'

We went together to reflect quietly in a church. Later, when he was far away from me, each time he had a premiere, Yves would send me the same telegram: 'Debut this evening. Go to church for me.'

But I've only prayed once like that, for the success of a friend, and it was for the triumph of the man I loved. I prayed for Marcel Cerdan to be world champion.

Finally Yves went on stage. It was October 1945. The whole of Paris had responded to my appeals and they were waiting in the auditorium of L'Etoile. I was in a box with the Montand family.

When he appeared under the spotlight there wasn't a murmur. Paris gave its new star an icy cold welcome. Yves began to sing. My throat was tight, my heart throbbed, I listened to him and I besought Heaven to help him for he deserved it.

When he had finished his last song he remained standing there in front of these people, who were still silent. He awaited the verdict. In my dressing room I was chewing my handkerchief into little pieces.

Suddenly there was applause for him, and cries of 'Bravo!' and shouting. It was a triumph. A triumph that was talked about for months. A triumph that will never be forgotten by those who were there.

That night I told myself that Yves Montand had perhaps forgiven me.

12

To Have Courage

There have been several fateful years in my life: 1949 . . .
the death of Marcel Cerdan; 1958 . . . 1960 . . . car
accidents, operations, illness taking hold of me. And also
several disappointments and broken relationships.

At times of misfortune or death, friends fade away, all
except the true ones. One day, not long ago, I had to make
a selection from among all those people who have
gravitated around me for so long and still do so. A rigorous
selection. To prevent myself suffering too much from the
ingratitude of some of them, I put them out of my mind and
out of my life. Yet I need friends around me, as many as
possible; without them I feel unsteady, I lose confidence in
myself. And then I can't sing any more. Now I need to sing
in order to live. Yes, twice over: in order to earn my living
and also because if I couldn't sing any more I couldn't exist
any longer, whatever my doctors sometimes think.

'Don't sing any more, Edith,' they beg me. 'You're
killing yourself!'

How many times have I heard those words! Every
time I stumbled and had to hold on to the piano or the
microphone. Every time in recent years that I collapsed on
stage. Every time an ambulance rushed me to Neuilly and
the American hospital. And still today. . . . But the idea of
not singing again, no, I can't accept it.

Yet one day I thought I was going to abandon

everything. I was fed up! I was frightened, so frightened of being finished, of never finding my voice again! I passed whole days lying prostrate on my bed, waiting for my strength to return, waiting for the strength I needed in order to sing.

I had reached such a state of weakness that I could no longer even lift the telephone receiver to my ear. As soon as I sat down the room, with the furniture and the objects in it, began to spin like a crazy roundabout. I felt hollow; my voice would crack as soon as I tried to sing a few bars. Even my laugh, my famous challenging laugh, was no more than a pitiful snigger. Friendship saved me. But the friendship of an unknown woman.

I was all alone in my apartment; I felt that everyone had forgotten me. Then the doorbell rang. I no longer remember how I had the strength to cross the drawing room and the hall and stand by the door to the landing. I opened the door myself. A young girl held out to me a bunch of violets; she was so nervous that she did not recognize me.

'For Madame Edith Piaf,' she murmured. Then she ran away.

I breathed in the scent of the little fresh flowers and I began to tremble. My eyes were blinded with tears; sobs choked me. All at once, I wanted, I needed to sing, yes, to sing for all my unknown friends, for my public, all those people who applaud me even before I've opened my mouth. These are my best friends, perhaps, those who will weep most sincerely when they follow me to the cemetery. . . if I haven't disappointed them before then! I don't want to disappoint them – I never wanted to do so. Often, to avoid disappointing them, I've even agreed to stake my entire health, unconditionally. I've overcome my worst moments of despair. And how I hated myself those evenings when, through my own fault, because I was taking drugs or because I'd drunk too much, I failed to give them the drug they wanted: my songs!

I had to sing: it's always been stronger than me, stronger than reason or caution.

Sometimes I look at old newspapers. I see pictures of myself being carried away in my impresario's arms, supported by my secretary, collapsing on a bed, pale, dishevelled, beaten.... And the captions under these pictures: Festival interrupted.... Piaf taken ill on stage.... Piaf exhausted.... Relapse.... Piaf's life in danger.... She is dying.... Removed to hospital urgently.... Another blood transfusion.... Piaf is killing herself by going on singing.

And I remember all the battles I've conducted against illness and death. Hard struggles, which I've had to conduct myself, despite the friends at my bedside.

But I was rewarded for my endurance. Only a few days later I could read other headlines: Piaf sang all the same!... Piaf's appearance on stage, was it a miracle? Yes, but also what a marvellous example of love, *joie de vivre*, courage!... She'll sing on to the end.... This little scrap of a woman, she's courage personified!

It's true that I've always wanted to have courage. They say that it's a masculine quality. But I believe that it's women who 'cope' best when things are going badly. It's a question of habit, especially for me. My apprenticeship in life was not particularly rosy.

But suddenly my courage fails slightly, because instead of talking about the past ... I have to talk about the present. The last chapter of my life. That sounds rather like a passing bell! Perhaps because I'm ill again today, and with each relapse I feel a little less attached to life, as though I'm grasping a rope over a precipice and it's inescapably wearing away.

No, I'm not pessimistic. I'm so happy with

Théo. . . . I ask nothing better than that it should last for a long time, a very long time. If all my happiness could be prolonged: Théo, my songs, success, recovery!

All the same, despite my belief in miracles, despite all those from which I've benefited for nearly half a century, all the time I've been here on earth – thirteen or fourteen already – I'm still obliged to look at myself in the mirror. This little puppet with her careful gait, her unco-ordinated gestures, her face that is prematurely aged. . . . I bear the unmistakable mark of someone who, alas, always comes to the rendezvous that has been arranged for her.

Yes, I need a lot of courage before I can talk about Théo Sarapo. The man who could have been the son I never had, the man who is only the man I love. One more? No, the last one. Unless he abandons me. . . .

I've only gone from one man to another because I've always looked for the same thing: for a man who would be really kind to me, gentle, affectionate, faithful. In reality, beneath my cynical exterior, despite my life story which cannot be recounted to children, I've got the heart of a shopgirl. But the day when I found that man, when he asked me to be his wife, when I had to say yes, I needed even more courage than I had needed to surmount every-thing else: poverty, illness and, worst of all, the ceaseless, pointless malevolence of envious people.

I knew too well what lay in store for us: scandal. Because Théo was twenty-seven and I was forty-seven. That was the scandal; that was what was going to cause all the gossip, the gibes, the insults, even.

But I had already experienced the gossip, the gibes and the insults. I was immune to them. Even the pity that came my way, I didn't care about it.

In my present state, when I know my life hangs by a thread, nothing which is not essential has any effect on me.

The essential thing is to love, to be loved, to be happy and in harmony with yourself.

Now I know that I was right to marry Théo: I'm happy. But if anyone thinks that I wanted that, if anyone believes that I said yes to this marriage without reflecting, without scruples, without remorse or apprehension, then they're thinking me sillier and crazier than I am.

The outcry that this disparate union caused could have broken me and my career, for ever. It could have ruined me. I didn't take this risk because, as some unkind people have alleged, the sales of my records had gone down and I had to make myself into a star again, by one means or another. The reason was much simpler than that, much more 'sensational'. Théo loved me. And I loved him – I still love him. . . . [1]

13

A Dream Makes the Choice for Me

The first time I saw him he didn't make a great impression on me. He came with one of my friends, who was visiting me. He sat down on the carpet in the salon and didn't say a word all evening. When he had gone, I thought, That young chap isn't very bright.

I saw him again in February 1962. I was suffering from double pneumonia. I'd been taken to hospital as a matter of urgency. Théo came to see me every day. He read novels to me, bought little dolls for me and also brought flowers.

It was then that our love developed. We got on well together. Nothing more; it was unexpected and therefore wonderful.

But how could I even have thought of marrying him? It's not credible, I told myself, and I took great care not to make any future plans. I was like someone in a train who suddenly discovers the landscape of his dreams, the ideal place where he would like to have lived and built his house. . . . But he knows that the train won't stop, and the landscape will disappear.

Théo will meet another woman, I thought, a woman of his own age. He'll make his life with her. It's normal. All the same, I'll have had that, his love!

I left the nursing home. He came to live nearby. One

day we were in the big drawing room in my apartment in the boulevard Lannes. It was still empty. Théo seemed to me unusually serious.

'What's the matter?' I asked him.

'If I asked you to marry me,' he replied, 'would you accept?'

I was so completely astonished that I broke into nervous laughter. But when I saw that Théo had gone white I controlled myself. I ran my fingers through his hair and explained to him in the kindest way possible, 'You're a young man, you've got all your life in front of you. One day you'll meet a younger woman. You're crazy.'

That didn't seem to console him, on the contrary.

'Listen,' I went on, 'a woman of my age doesn't marry just like that, in a casual way. She hasn't got the right, nor the time, to make a mistake, especially after the kind of life I've had. I'm asking you for time to think it over.'

He agreed. 'Very well, I'll wait for your answer for as long as it takes.'

I made him wait a month! Not a single day of that month went by without my thinking about this proposal of marriage. Of course I loved Théo. I felt an infinite tenderness towards him, and he was so gentle with me. I admit too that I felt rather proud to have made the conquest of a young man of his age. But marrying him?

Shortly before I met Théo I had had an argument with my friend Françoise because she had fallen in love with a boy younger than herself. And now this had happened to me! I had told her she was crazy, thoughtless. I had even said to her, 'Aren't you ashamed of going down the street with a boy who could be your son? Aren't you upset by the way people look at you?' And now in my turn. . . .

It was my pride that rebelled. At night I spent hours in the dark with my eyes wide open, wondering, Should I marry him? He's so good, so attentive! I shall never find another boy like him. But five minutes afterwards I would say to myself, Think carefully, Edith! In ten years' time you'll be fifty-seven and you'll be an old woman, while he'll be only thirty-seven, a man in the prime of life. At that moment, what will you represent for him? A terrible burden, perhaps. . . .

There was also another reason which tipped the balance towards a refusal. . . . Marriage frightened me. I had the feeling that I wasn't made for it, the impression that I lacked the qualities necessary to make a good wife. I'd never known how to look after a home, how to cook. Furniture, carpets, ornaments. . . those sort of things don't really interest me.

And then my first marriage, although it was more 'normal', had been a failure, despite the love that we felt for each other. And Jacques had also been kind, very understanding and very patient. But our profession had defeated our love. Now Théo is singing; Théo will act in films; Théo will have a career of his own. . . .

On the day of my divorce I had sworn never to go through such an experience again. . . . What was the point in getting married if a few years later I was to find myself more solitary than ever?

And there was something worse! Was I even capable of making a man happy? Was it still possible that I could succeed in accomplishing that task: to ensure a man's happiness?

I've always had an impossible character. I've been capricious and jealous. And whenever I'm jealous I fly into a terrible rage. In fact I don't tolerate a man's will very easily. I'm tempted to impose my will on him. I'm a restive type of person and I possess the spirit of contradiction in an extreme form.

In making an honest list of the reasons for and against, I could see clearly that as far as this marriage was concerned there were more reasons against it.

And yet I said yes to Théo. It was a dream that decided me. Basing your life on a dream is something that always surprises the sceptics, but our entire life is made up of chance happenings, good or bad, against which human will is virtually powerless.

Until now my dreams had given me good advice and judicious warnings. Why should I not have listened to this one? Had I not reached a point in my life when I had very little to lose and everything to gain? Among other things the wonderful presence of a man who was young, handsome and strong, a man who showed extraordinary kindness towards me. When he comes to close my eyes, something which in my present state of health is a possibility I must consider, his hands will be gentle.

I have already told you about the dream in which the telephone rings and nobody speaks when I answer . . . that dream which predicts to me faithfully that the love between a man and myself is about to die. . . .

Every night following Théo's marriage proposal, I waited for the bad dream to come back. Would it be tonight, tomorrow night, the night after tomorrow? Nearly a month had passed; it must have been the last day of June. In my sleep the telephone rang, I lifted the receiver . . . and for the first time a voice replied to my anguished 'hello'.

That voice was the voice of Théo.

But I was still not convinced. I said to myself, Who are you to believe that you still have a right to happiness? A woman who has made a collection of lovers and unhappy loves. You have ruined your health by hanging around bars all night, never following the orders the doctors imposed on you. You're exhausted; you're more worn out than any other woman your age. Result: the slightest draught makes you take to your bed for a week, the slightest distance you walk exhausts you. If you depart from your diet even a little

103

you're ill for several days and each time it takes you longer to recover your strength.

I said to myself, You've done too many stupid things in your life! You've earned an entire fortune but you've thrown it away, often stupidly. Instead of having a welcoming and well-furnished apartment, not even the piano in your salon belongs to you.

At forty-seven I found myself just the same as I was the day when I was sixteen and left my father to go singing in the streets. That is to say, alone. With fewer illusions, fewer hopes and less strength.

How can all that end except in catastrophe? Death would be less of a disaster.

But suppose you suddenly found yourself a little old lady, without talent, financially ruined...dependent on other people, you who until now usually took charge of others?

My assessment ended when I discovered that I was bankrupt to such an extent that I finally found myself overwhelmed with scruples. This young man, whose life was just beginning, did I have the right to make him share what remained of mine: so much ruin, so much degeneration?

To counterbalance all this there was the dream. When dawn came the sound of the telephone was still ringing in my ears. Then all my scruples vanished. After all, was I not going to love him more than any other woman could love him?

Soon I was waiting for Théo as though I were an impatient young girl. When he again asked me to marry him, I hesitated no longer. I said yes.

Je ne regrette rien. I love him. If that shocks anyone, it can't surprise them. What woman of my age would not be dazzled by the love of a man *his* age?

Besides, when I analyse this love, I find not only the

love of a woman for a man, but also another feeling that life has denied me until now: maternal love. Théo, with his laughter, his drive and his youth, sometimes makes me feel like I have a son. In the most sensual of mistresses there is always a mother concealed from view. Only those who see wrong in everything will be offended.

I myself know that my love for Théo is something of which I need not feel ashamed. If that had been the case, would I have dared, a few days later, to go to Lisieux to ask a favour from the saint who had restored my sight to me when I was a child?[1] No! That would have been sacrilege.

We knelt down, Théo and I, in front of her statue and I begged her, 'Grant me a few more years of the happiness I've just discovered, the happiness I've waited for all my life.'

I don't know if these years will be granted to me. What I do know is that however short they are, even if there is only one, or even just a few months of happiness, I shall always thank Providence. I no longer deserved that happiness. I no longer believed in it.

14

Je n'en connais pas la fin

From the moment I said yes to the day when the Orthodox priest placed the wedding crowns on our heads, anguish did not spare me. For this reason I was literally panic-stricken at something Théo said to me one day: 'I have to ask my father if he agrees to my marrying you.'

That may seem ridiculous to some people, but for me the consent of his parents was very important. I hoped I would be allowed into his family and received with joy. In fact Théo had admitted to me that his father was a man with very strict ideas about marriage.

It's going to be terrible, I thought, when Théo announces to them that he wants to marry a woman old enough to be his mother!

'Obviously, Edith,' Théo had reassured me, 'even if my father refuses, I shall marry you all the same.'

But my pleasure would have been lacklustre. I would have thought for the rest of my life that I had stolen a son from his parents. I knew only too well what it was like to live without father or mother! For that reason my heart was in my boots the day Théo took me to his father's house – it was July 26, 1962. He felt the same, in fact. I said to myself: If his father refuses, I shall consider that it is a sign from the gods. It will mean that I no longer deserve happiness.

We went by car to La Frette, where his parents live.

During the drive, Théo and I did not exchange a single word. He held my hand in his; he smiled at me but he was anxious.

Eventually we arrived. In the small drawing room were his mother, his father and his two younger sisters, Christie and Cathy. They all smiled at me. But we were all terribly tense.

It was Cathy who broke the ice. She suddenly stood up and put on a record: twist music. Christie asked me if I knew how to dance it. I said I didn't. Then the two girls replied, 'Come on, we'll teach you.'

And there I was in the middle of the drawing room twisting like a teenager with those two young things.

All at once I saw Théo go out into the garden with his mother and father. I thought, That's it, it's happening now. I shivered with fright – I wanted to run away – but the record went on playing, blaring out pop music.

Through the window I could see Théo in discussion with his parents. It seemed to me that time was standing still. And they all looked so serious! I thought that Monsieur Lamboukas was not in agreement. It would hardly have been surprising!

Finally they all came back in, their heads lowered, walking slowly. I was convinced that things were not going well and tears came to my eyes.

When they were back in the drawing room Monsieur Lamboukas looked at me in silence for a long moment. Then he spoke to me. 'Théo has asked me for permission to marry you,' he said. 'He is a respectful son. But he's free, and he's old enough to know what he's doing. That is no concern of mine. Now, all the same, I'd like you to know: I am very happy to receive you into my family.'

I made a great effort to force back my tears. Then Théo's mother, who is eight months younger than I am, spoke to me: 'Edith, call me *maman*!'

It was too much; I began to cry. Once the emotional scene was over we had a cheerful dinner. People for whom family life is normal, everyday life, will probably find it hard to understand the extent of my happiness. For the first time in my existence I was sitting in the midst of a father, a mother, two sisters and . . . my future husband. And I forgot my age! I had become once more that little girl who had dreamed day after day about this uneventful happiness!

I was overwhelmed too by the affection which this father and mother felt for their son. Until then I had not been sure that maternal and paternal love really existed.

When Monsieur Lamboukas took me aside to express his anxiety about Théo and his career, I had to face the facts. This man had worked all his life for his wife and children. He had hoped that Théo would succeed him as director of his hairdressing salon. And Théo was now taking up a crowded and uncertain profession, that of a singer!

'But I've never wanted to stop him from trying his luck. Only you can tell him if he has talent or not,' he told me.

And the affection Théo's mother showed! How could I fail to be moved to tears as I saw her, I, who had been abandoned as a baby two months old!

'Our home is yours now,' she told me.

Before I left *maman* gave me a large packet. Apricots and peaches gathered in her garden . . .the finest jewels in the world could not have given me as much pleasure as this humble fruit!

From that day I spent all my Sundays at La Frette with Théo. After lunch *maman* Lamboukas and I would sit on a divan and while she knitted, I would do embroidery or tapestry work. She never stopped talking to me about her Théo. She told me about the games and silly jokes he had played when he was little; she told me about the nineteen months he had spent in Algeria, whence he returned thinner by twenty-five pounds.

On the day of our engagement, which we celebrated at La Frette, we fixed the date of our wedding: October 9.

My future mother-in-law began to cry and I misunderstood the reason for her tears. I asked her outright: 'Are you upset by the difference in age between Théo and me? Be frank with me!'

She looked at me affectionately. 'You can make a very happy couple,' she said. 'Obviously my Théo is still an overgrown boy. He's boisterous and rowdy. But I know that he loves you with all his heart. Age doesn't affect that at all. You'll see, Edith, you will complete each other.'

His sisters also behaved towards me in an adorable way.

I knew that this marriage would earn me jeers and insults, that perhaps even my public would desert me, in which case I would be ruined. . . . But in the end everyone seemed pleased at the idea of the marriage!

In spite of that, my anxiety increased as I saw the date of the wedding come gradually closer. I was obsessed by those two figures: forty-seven . . . twenty-seven. . . . My age, Théo's age. Forty-seven . . . twenty-seven.

Time went by. The day of the civil ceremony dawned. In two hours I would be appearing on Théo's arm before the Registrar in order to sign the marriage register.

Théo had just done my hair and I was about to fix my make-up. I had already put on my black silk dress. I was sitting in front of my mirror. It was then that I burst into tears. I felt desperate. I threw myself on my bed.

Théo came to me at once. 'What's the matter?' he stammered.

'No,' I muttered, 'I can't marry you. It's madness. It's painful for you today, but later you'll thank me.'

He was disconcerted; he thought I had gone crazy. 'But why, why?' he repeated mechanically.

Then I turned towards him, my ravaged face wet with tears. 'Look at me!' I screamed. 'I'm a wreck, not a woman, just a poor wretch who can't even stand up! You can't marry someone like that.' And I told him the truth about the week I'd just lived through. A week of horrible suffering that I had jealously concealed from him.

It had all begun during the night of October 3 – 4. I had woken up screaming with pain. I felt as if my right wrist and my feet were being crushed. It was a new attack of rheumatoid arthritis.

Despite my pain I had not wanted to wake Théo. I let him sleep in peace in his room at the other end of the apartment. I didn't want to worry him! I got up and telephoned my doctor. I begged him to come at once. I had reached the end of my physical and mental endurance.

When he rang my doorbell a few moments later I dragged myself there and opened the door myself, but I nearly fainted into his arms, the effort had been so painful. After a rapid examination he gave me a strong dose of cortisone to ease my pain and then a sleeping pill. He waited there for an hour until I was asleep.

The next day I said nothing to Théo. Although I was exhausted I sang that evening at the Olympia, with him. As soon as I came home I went to bed. The pain returned, piercing my body. Rheumatoid arthritis is a horrible thing. But I still wanted to get married. Two days later, thank God, my rheumatic attack was over. It was three days before the ceremony.

I felt my strength returning, but I had not yet come to the end of my problems!

In fact that day, I don't know where or how, I caught a chill. All night I shivered, and when I tried to get up I collapsed on the floor. Then I really had to call Théo to help me.

He was terribly upset. 'What's the matter, Edith? What's happened?'

I tried to cheat again. I told him that it was nothing, that I just had a cold and there was no need to make it into a drama.

I insisted to my doctor that he must hide the truth from Théo. Poor doctor! He was in a quandary. He didn't dare argue with me, but neither was he very pleased that nobody was keeping an eye on me. In any case he insisted that I should stay at home in bed until my wedding, otherwise he would take no responsibility for anything.

But I have always believed that 'an ill weed grows apace'. The next evening, instead of staying in the warm, I had myself driven to the Olympia and I sang. Théo's presence galvanized me. But I came back to the apartment in a pitiful state. I had to be supported. I couldn't walk. I couldn't talk. I was shivering. I felt feverish and frozen at the same time. When at last I had been put to bed I became delirious, or so I learned later.

Those were the memories that came back to me two hours before I was due to become Madame Lamboukas!

One last time I reproached myself: It's true, we love each other, but my life now is hanging by a thread. Isn't it totally wrong to attach to myself this young man who has all his life in front of him, who's healthy and strong?

'I'm afraid I can't make you happy,' I told him. 'Everything's against us.'

He interrupted me. He had taken me by the shoulders, and his voice was hard: 'I want to marry you. I want you to bear my name. If you're afraid of not making me happy, I'm afraid of losing you. I don't want you to think about your health any longer . . . apart from deciding to look after yourself properly at last. I'll look after you. It's the role of a husband to be there when his wife's ill. You say your health is fragile? I know. So what? Weren't you ill when I told you I loved you? Everyone had abandoned you, apart from the few friends who remained faithful, those who've stayed by you. I was disgusted when so many of them disappeared. That's how I realized I loved you, that I wanted you to be happy.' Théo was launched. He wouldn't let me argue. 'You don't want to let me waste my time because I'm young? I've spent enough time staying out all night. At twenty-seven, it's time I started enriching my life, time that I dedicate myself to someone. I want that someone to be you.'

If any woman, even a young woman, even someone bursting with health, is capable of resisting a declaration like that, then I no longer know anything about women, about life and most of all about love!

I didn't cry any more. But within myself I asked to be forgiven. You don't deserve this, I repeated to myself. You've ruined so many chances of happiness, destroyed so many lives, starting with your own.

But Théo knew that he had already won the battle. He had recovered that smile that I could not resist. He dried my eyes and scolded me. 'I shall have to do your hair again,' he said suddenly. 'Be quick. They'll soon be waiting for us. We won't go away on our honeymoon tonight, we'll sing, together! But as soon as we've finished our recital at the Olympia I'll take you to Greece.'

After that everything went very quickly. It had to, in fact. All my cheerful songs – I do have some – were singing within me. The doctor came. I was given vitamins and stimulants.

I left on Théo's arm. In the street I had one last dizzy spell. Those people who were waiting for me. . . . No, they didn't whistle at me! Chanting, they called for us to appear on the balcony of the mairie of the 16th arrondissement:

'Long live Edith, long live Théo!'

At that moment I stopped being afraid of the future, of what might happen to me. Through clenched teeth I murmured, for myself alone:

> *Peut m'arriver n'importe quoi*
> *Ça m'est égal*
> *Peut m'arriver n'importe quoi*
> *Je m'en fous pas mal.* . . . [1]

I was happy, and ready. Ready for the rest of my life, even if, as in one of my other songs:

> *Je n'en connais pas la fin.* . . . [2]

That end lay not far ahead. Théo decided to send his ailing wife to the Côte d'Azur for a rest, supervised by a nurse. He took a villa at St Jean Cap Ferrat, then a smaller one near Mougins and finally a house in a village called Plascassier, near Grasse. Old friends such as Raymond Asso came to see the convalescent; other visitors included her songwriters, her two young sisters-in-law and her own half-sister, Denise Gassion, with whom she had had little contact. Jean Cocteau, who was in Paris and ill himself, telephoned often. If she recovered enough to start making plans for the future, she also asked for candles to be lit to St Rita, patron of lost causes.

She died shortly after 1 p.m. on October 10, 1963. Her body was transported in secret to Paris, for the star so closely associated with *la Ville Lumière* could not be allowed to die in an obscure Provençal village. The announcement was made in Paris and some two million people followed the funeral procession to Père Lachaise.

Théo Sarapo attempted to pay his wife's debts. He died in 1970 after a car accident near Limoges.

In September 1981 Jacques Chirac, mayor of Paris, inaugurated the Place Edith Piaf in the 20th arrondissement, near Belleville, where she had been born.

M.C.

Notes

Chapter 1
1 *La môme Piaf*, literally the kid sparrow, was Edith's early stage name, given to her by Louis Leplée.

Chapter 2
1 Edith never forgave her mother for abandoning her when she was a few months old. This mother, Anetta Giovanna Maillard, born in Italy of partly North African origin, had married Edith's father in 1914, when he was in the army. Their daughter was born on December 19, 1915 and named Edith after the courageous British nurse Edith Cavell. Her birth took place at the famous old Hôpital Tenon in the rue de Chine, in the faubourg of Ménilmontant, and not on the pavement in the rue de Belleville, as so often stated. This was the first of the many Piaf legends and those who wish to believe it may of course do so. Piaf herself certainly believed it. Outside no. 115 in this long old street is a plaque, unveiled by Maurice Chevalier, commemorating the legend as truth.

Anetta Maillard was not interested in domesticity or in her baby. She had been used to a nomadic life in circuses and fairgrounds. Calling herself Line Marsa she left her husband and went to sing in the streets. Some sixteen years later her daughter Edith did the same thing.

Louis Gassion had been born in Normandy and his mother Louise still lived there. She worked as a cook in a brothel run by a Gassion cousin in Bernay, situated between Lisieux and Evreux. Edith was sent there by her father and stayed for several years.
2 For Raymond Asso and the song *Mon légionnaire*, see note 4, Chapter 3.
3 Edith's years in *le milieu*, the Paris underworld, probably explain why so many of her successful songs evoke the violent, unhappy lives of poor people, and in particular the unhappiness of young women. They were forced into menial jobs and had little chance of escaping into a more comfortable existence.

Chapter 3
1 Gerny's Club was situated southwest of the Champs-Elysées, near the Arc de Triomphe.
2 The police station on the Quai des Orfèvres is well known to admirers of Simenon's Inspector Maigret.

3   Leplée's murder was never solved. Fortunately Edith was able to furnish an alibi, for the police regarded her as a prime suspect.

4   Raymond Asso helped to create Piaf. He had been born in Nice in 1901, worked as a shepherd in Morocco and, after serving in the Middle East in a regiment of spahis, had run a factory in France. He enjoyed writing poems and was lucky enough to meet the composer Marguerite Monnot, for she set many of them to music. Edith seemed to believe that he wrote *Mon légionnaire* for her after hearing about her legionnaire lover. In fact the song was created by the famous music hall artist Marie Dubas, who sang it with great success. But later generations will always associate it with Piaf, who recorded her emotional rendering of it in 1937.

It has to be said that she treated Asso very badly.

5   Paul Meurisse was the son of a banker in the provinces and gave up a career in law after winning a song competition at the Alhambra music hall in Paris. The stormy life he lived with Piaf was used by Jean Cocteau in the short play *Le bel indifférent*, which the poet wrote for the couple, and in 1940 they acted it successfully at Les Bouffes parisiens. It was in fact a monologue for Edith, since Meurisse, as her lover, remains silent throughout. She told him he acted better than he sang, and in fact he later became an actor.

6   Piaf had been deeply impressed by John Garfield's acting when she saw him in *Hamlet*.

Chapter 4

1   For Piaf's second husband, Théo, see Chapters 12–14.

2   Marcel Cerdan, who was a year younger than Edith, was born in Sidi-bel-Abbès in Algeria, the original home of the Foreign Legion. His father was Spanish, his mother French. When Marcel was seven the family moved to Morocco. He took up boxing and in 1939 won the European middleweight championship in Milan. He first met Edith at the Club des Cinq in Paris but the couple came closer when they met again in New York in 1947. The press were bribed to say nothing about the relationship. In 1948 Cerdan defeated Tony Zale in New York, becoming world middleweight champion. The following year he lost the title to Jake La Motta and the boxing world blamed Edith for wasting his time and energy.

Edith always idealized this relationship because Cerdan's early death came before there had been time for any deterioration.

3   Piaf should have said *near* Lisieux. She was at Bernay, some fifteen

miles to the west.

4   Edith enjoyed 'educating' her friends and lovers. Jack London's autobiographical novel *Martin Eden* of 1909 was one of her favourite books, for it told of a self-educated man and his attempt to cope with success. She saw something of her own story in this.

5   Edith gave all her lovers new suits, shoes, etc., but it was unkindly said that her choice was no better than the tastes she criticized.

6   For more about Edith's addiction to spiritualism, see Chapter 7.

7   Marcel Cerdan Junior played the part of his father in the Claude Lelouch film of 1983, *Edith et Marcel*.

Chapter 5

1   There was probably no one person called Janine. Many people, friends and non-friends, procured drugs for Piaf.

2   The 'Supercircus' tour was a disaster and many performances were cancelled. It ended in the northwest, not far from Nantes.

3   Piaf's unhappy mother, Line Marsa, indeed died alone in 1945. Her body was made into a parcel by a fellow tenant and put out into the street until the local morgue sent a van to take it away.

Chapter 6

1   Edith had, in succession, two lovers who were both champion cyclists. Of André Pousse, with whom she lived for a year, she says nothing. The man who took possessions from the family home into Edith's apartment was Louis ('Toto') Gérardin.

2   Jacques Pills was nicknamed 'Monsieur Charme'. He had come into the theatre by way of the Casino de Paris and soon formed a successful singing partnership with Georges Tabet. Their best-known song, *Couchés dans le foin*, lasted so long that it was later recorded by the Andrews sisters as *Lying in the Hay*. Pills had previously been married to the singer Lucienne Boyer. The civil marriage took place in Paris in June 1952 at the mairie of the 16th arrondissement. Piaf wanted a church wedding later but may have forgotten that the church she chose, that of St Vincent de Paul in the Chelsea area of New York, was the same one where she had lit candles in memory of Marcel Cerdan.

3   Jacques Pills gave a somewhat different account of how he came to marry Piaf. He said *he* was ready for marriage, but she must ask herself if *she* was ready.

4   Douglas Davis made two contributions to Edith's life. He taught her to swim, but more importantly he painted some extraordinary

portraits of her, which bring out strongly the feeling of underlying tragedy in so much of her singing.

5   Edith does not name the man who treated her so badly, but it can be assumed that she is referring to Georges Moustaki. See also Chapter 10, p. 81.

Chapter 7

1   Intellectual admirers of Piaf find it hard to accept her belief in superstition and the occult, but it was an essential part of her nature. She was often tricked by others into believing that her seance table was sending her messages, and when André Pousse was living with her he decided he would end this unreal way of life. He broke up the table with his own hands.

2   Charles Dumont was important to Edith during the last three years of her life, for he composed her great success, *Non, je ne regrette rien*, and many other songs. Eddie Constantine, her first lover after the death of Cerdan, was best known later as a screen actor and appeared with her in the musical comedy *La p'tite Lili* in 1951. Leveillé, a Canadian, composed a few songs for her. She attempted to make Félix Marten into a star, provided he sang love songs, but their association was short-lived. Michel Rivegauche and Henri Contet were brilliant librettists. Marguerite Monnot composed the music for sixty or so Piaf songs. Sadly, she died at the age of thirty-one, but will surely be remembered for *Irma la douce*, an international success, as well as for her contribution to Piaf's repertoire. Piaf condescends here to add a mention of Moustaki, who at least wrote the words for *Milord* in 1959. The following year her recording of this song held seventeenth place for two weeks in the British Top Twenty. (I myself was touched to realize that my own initials might have given me a favoured if minor place among the M and the C people.)

Chapter 8

1   Ginette Richer was a faithful companion to Piaf for some years.

Chapter 9

1   This is one of the most melodramatic chapters in all Piaf's recollections and contradicts her earlier claim that she *did* sell herself for ten francs. Jean Noli wrote that he advised her against telling the latter version, which he thought might upset her fans.

The sad, brief story of little Marcelle is perpetuated by the addition of her name on Piaf's splendid, if hideous, tomb in the cemetery of Père Lachaise.

Chapter 11

1 There were in fact nine men in the group Les Compagnons de la Chanson. Their leader, Jean-Louis Jaubert, was Piaf's lover for a time.

2 Piaf's training of Yves Montand is a well-known story, and he was surely one of her greatest successes. They appeared together in a 1946 film, *Etoile sans Lumière*, her favourite among the few films she made. Piaf deserted Montand when she thought she could teach him nothing more, but his later wife, Simone Signoret, said that he was deeply upset by the break.

Chapter 12

1 Piaf's relationship with Theophanis Lamboukas, whom she called Théo Sarapo, adapting his surname from the Greek word for love, moved quickly. She met him first early in 1962 and a few months later, when she had fallen in love with him, decided she would make him into a singer. By July that year she wanted favourable articles in the press about their association; according to Jean Noli it was thought that the announcement of their marriage would supply useful publicity following her recovery from her recent illness.

This announcement was made in August, when Piaf sang in several towns along the Côte d'Azur. Théo sang with her that brilliant and touching duet *A quoi ça sert l'amour*, which seemed to summarize her life: the last lover was the first lover, nobody before mattered, now all was well. At the same time there was another new Piaf song, *Le Droit d'aimer*, the right to love: she had won this right at the risk of destroying herself, nothing would stop her from loving. . . . And indeed nothing did. She also made Théo into a presentable singer, even if his voice was slightly too nasal, and wrote several songs for him. The latest Piaf romance was reported in Britain, although she had told a *Daily Express* reporter that the English didn't understand about falling in love.

After the wedding in October the bride went through another detoxification cure, and was just well enough to undertake a short tour of Belgium and Holland. In February 1963 she sang at the Bobino music hall in Paris, her last public appearance, and her last recording was made two months later.

Chapter 13

1 Piaf believed the legend that she had been blind as a child and that St Thérèse had cured her. It is generally assumed that she suffered briefly from conjunctivitis.

Chapter 14
1   Anything can happen now
           And I'll just close the door
           Anything can happen now
           For I don't care any more. . . .
2   I cannot see the end. . . .